NOT ASIAN ENOUGH

A GRAPHIC NOVEL BY ALEXANDRA LAI

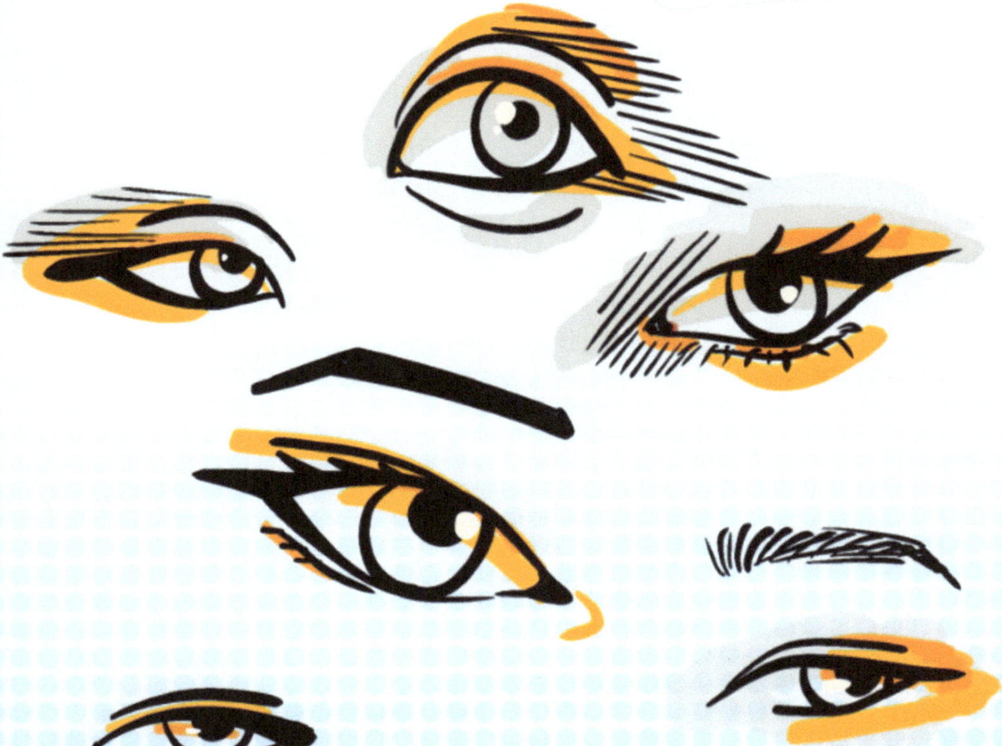

CERTAIN NAMES IN THE STORY HAVE BEEN ALTERNATED
FOR PRIVACY

A BIG THANKS TO MR. MORRIS (MY JUNIOR
YEAR ART TEACHER) FOR TEACHING ME HOW
TO MAKE A BOOK FOR SECOND-GRADERS.
THIS PUBLISHING EXPERIENCE HELPED ME
LEARN THE BASICS OF BOOK-MAKING.

AN EVEN BIGGER THANKS TO MY FAMILY AND
FRIENDS WHO NEVER DOUBTED MY ABILITY TO
MAKE THIS BOOK, WHO WILL MOST LIKELY
BUY MULTIPLE COPIES OF THIS.

CHAPTER 1:
BEFORE TAIWAN

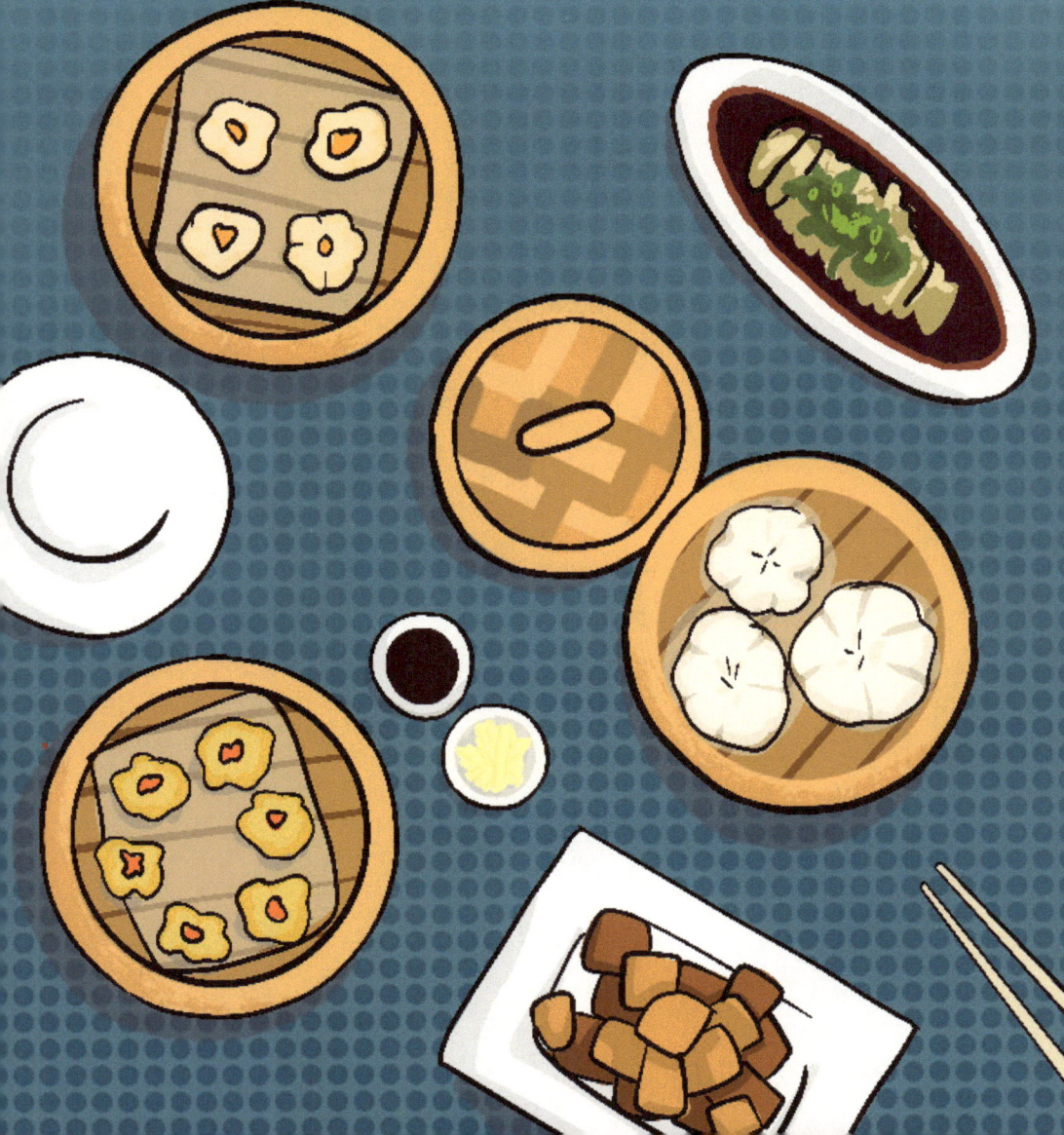

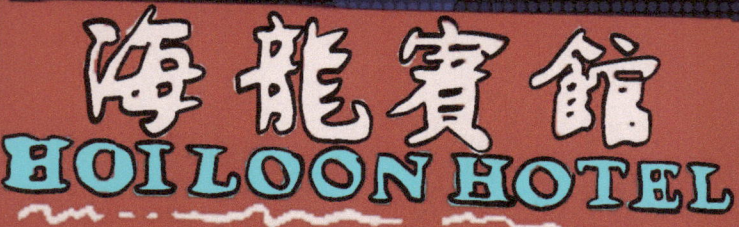

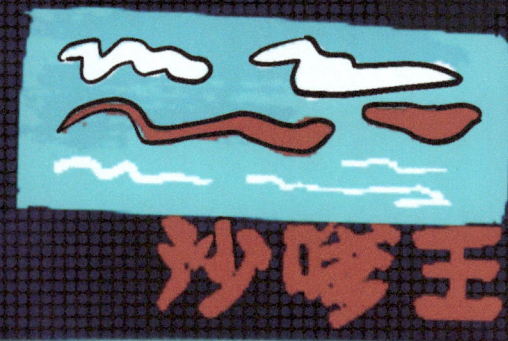

UP UNTIL 8TH GRADE, I HAD BEEN LIVING IN HONG KONG FOR AS LONG AS I COULD REMEMBER

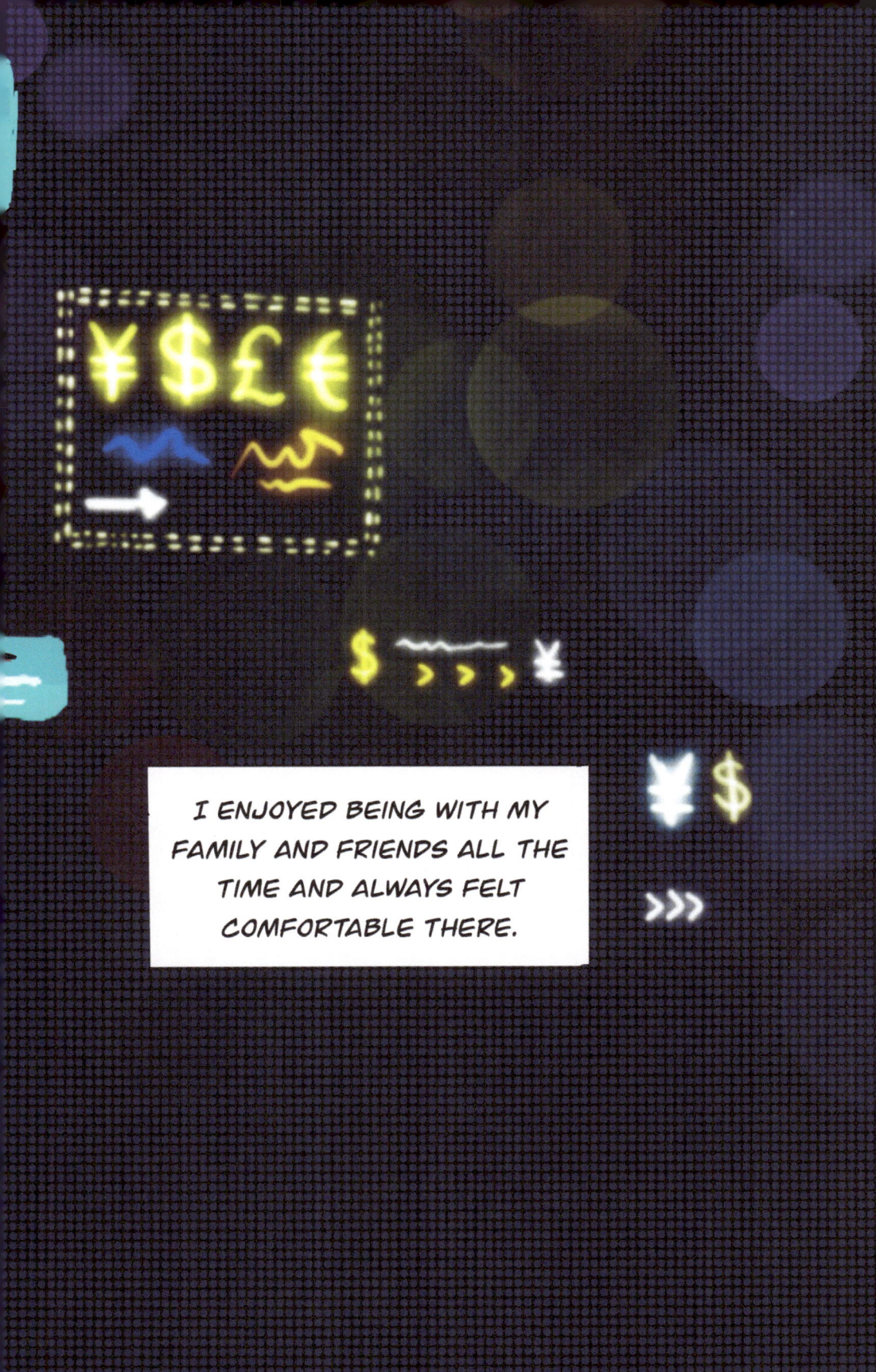

I ENJOYED BEING WITH MY FAMILY AND FRIENDS ALL THE TIME AND ALWAYS FELT COMFORTABLE THERE.

HOWEVER, SINCE MY SCHOOL IN HONG KONG WAS SCARED OF CHINA INVADING ONE DAY, THEY FORBADE STUDENTS FROM SPEAKING CANTONESE AND DEMANDED THAT WE SPEAK MANDARIN.

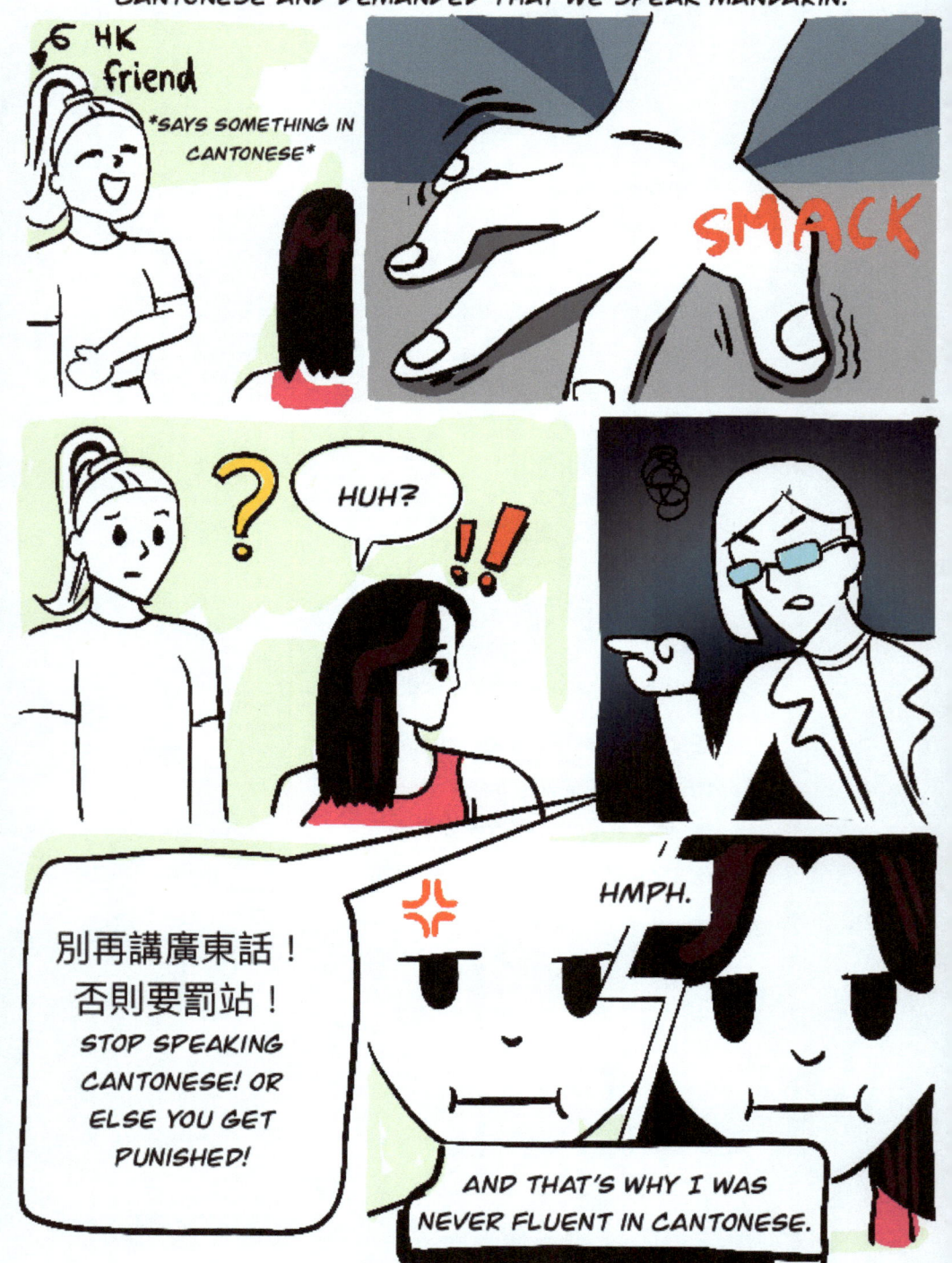

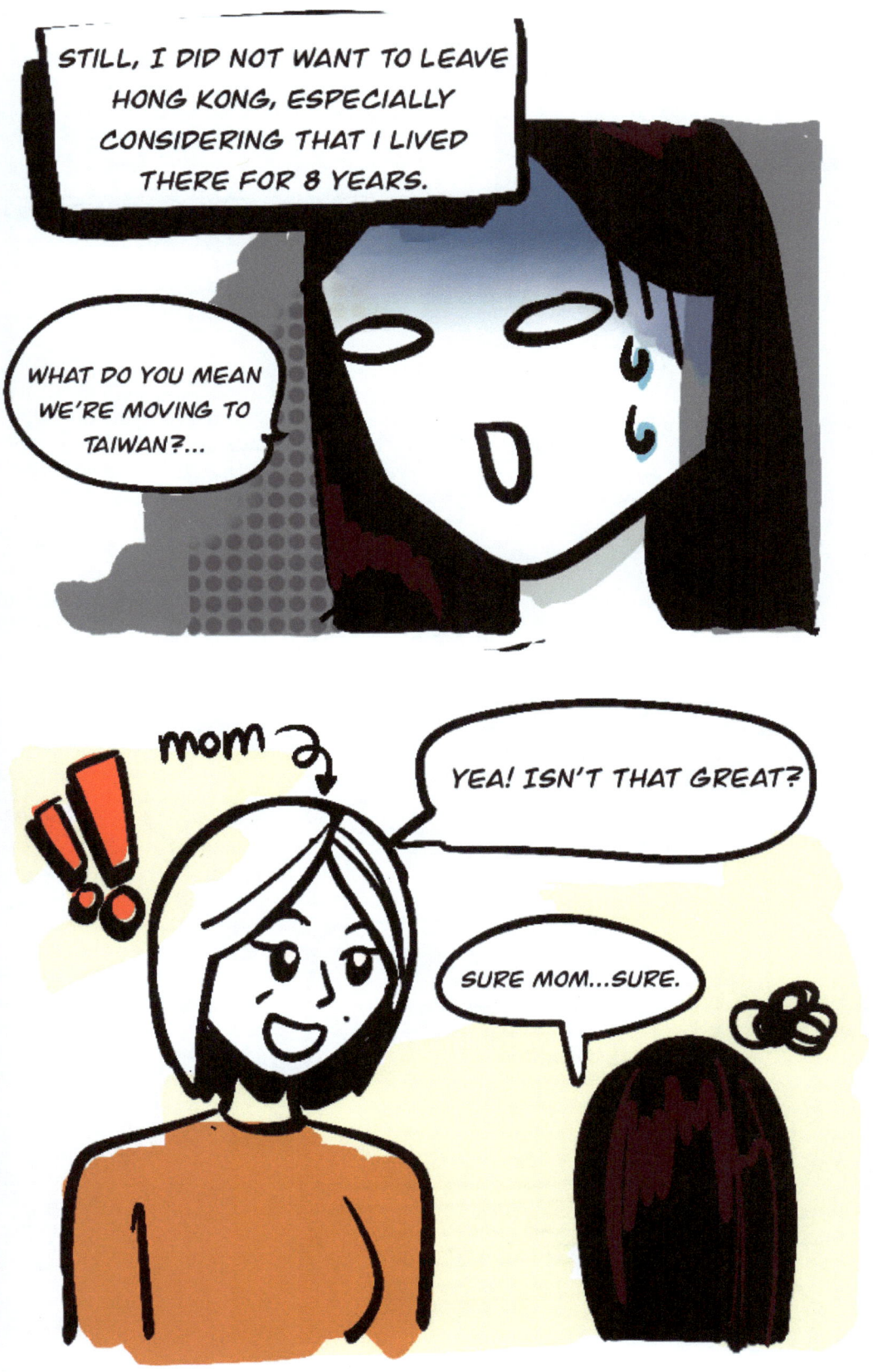

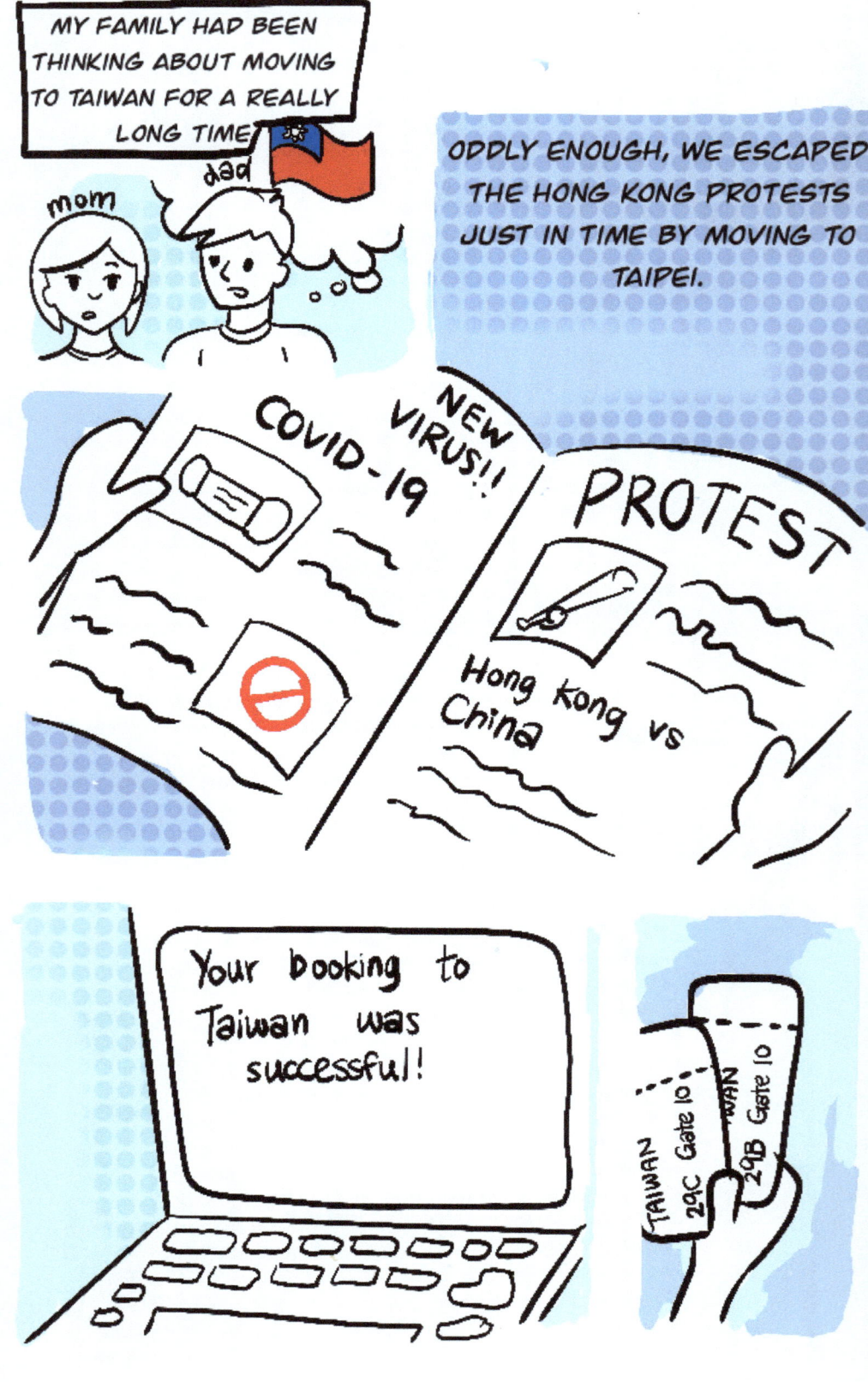

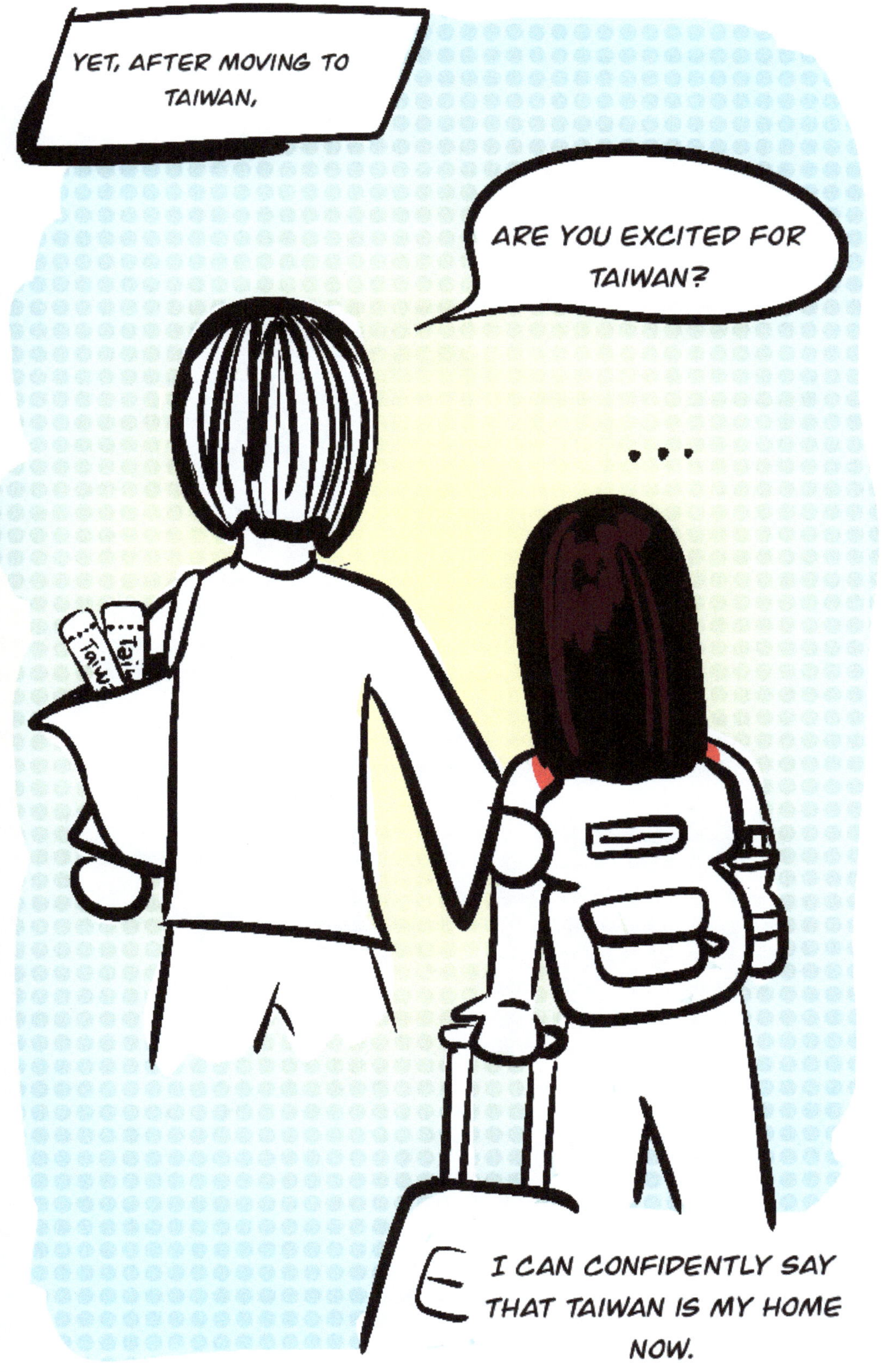
YET, AFTER MOVING TO TAIWAN,
ARE YOU EXCITED FOR TAIWAN?
...
I CAN CONFIDENTLY SAY THAT TAIWAN IS MY HOME NOW.

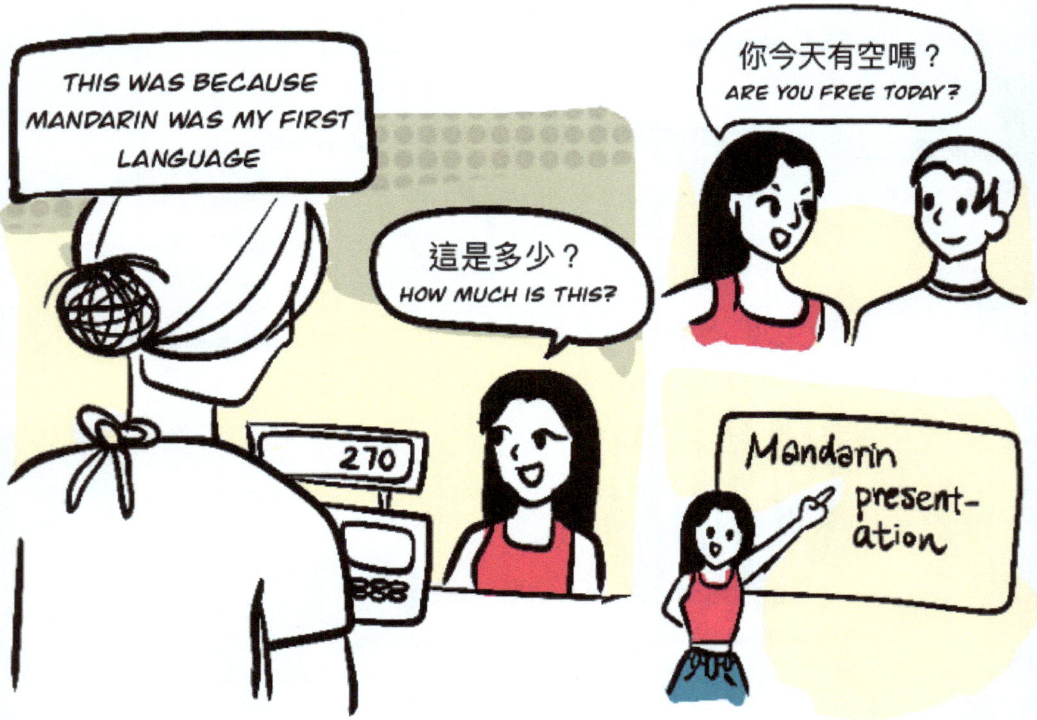

This was because Mandarin was my first language

這是多少？
How much is this?

270

你今天有空嗎？
Are you free today?

Mandarin present-ation

So, I naturally felt less foreign and got around easier in Taiwan, a place that purely speaks Mandarin.

帶我去台北101
Take me to the Taipei 101 building

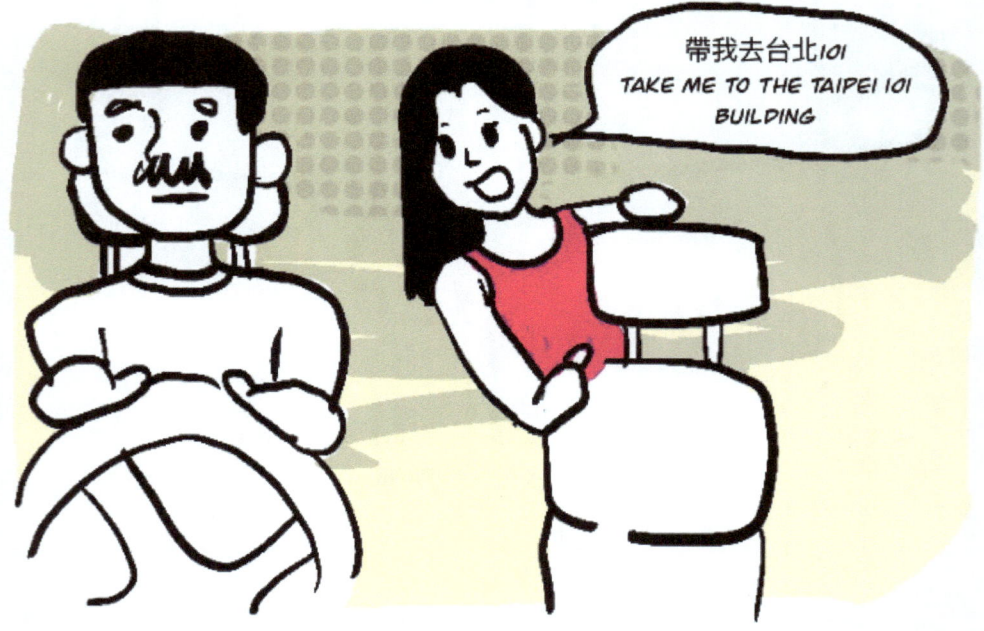

CHAPTER 2: MOVING TO TAIWAN

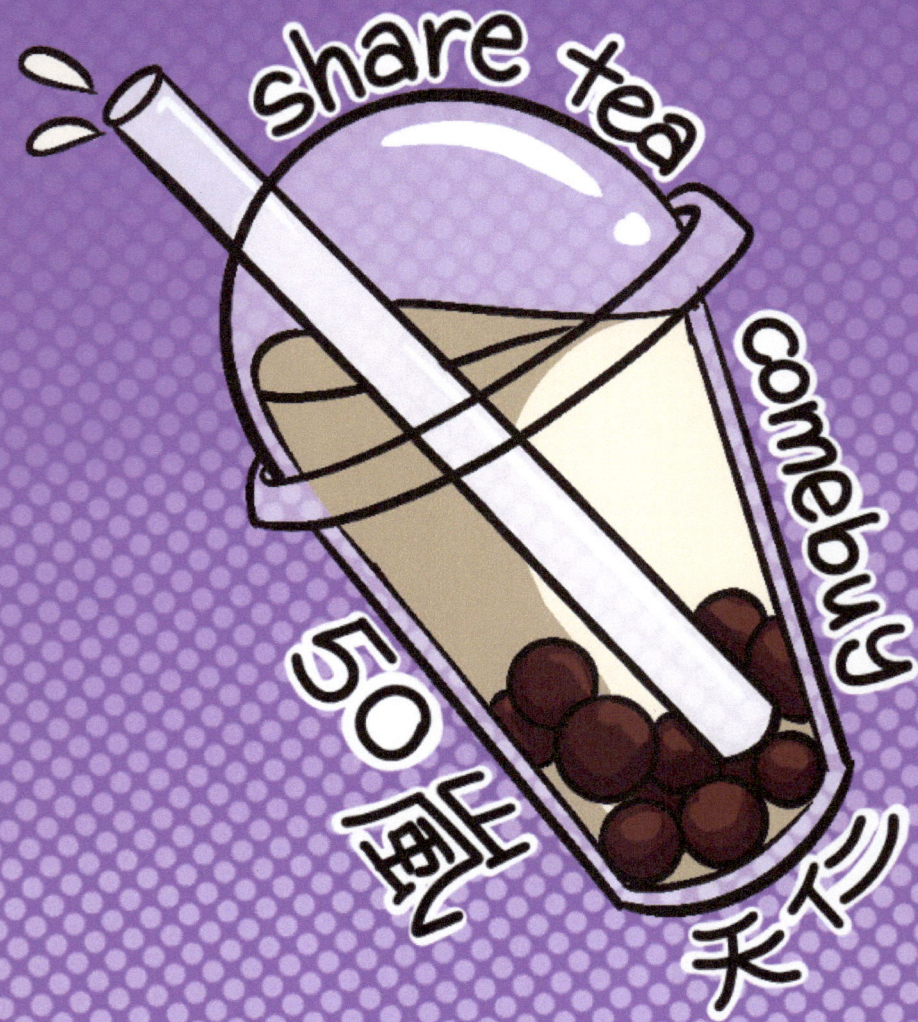

INTRODUCTION TO TAIWAN:
DAD'S PARENTS

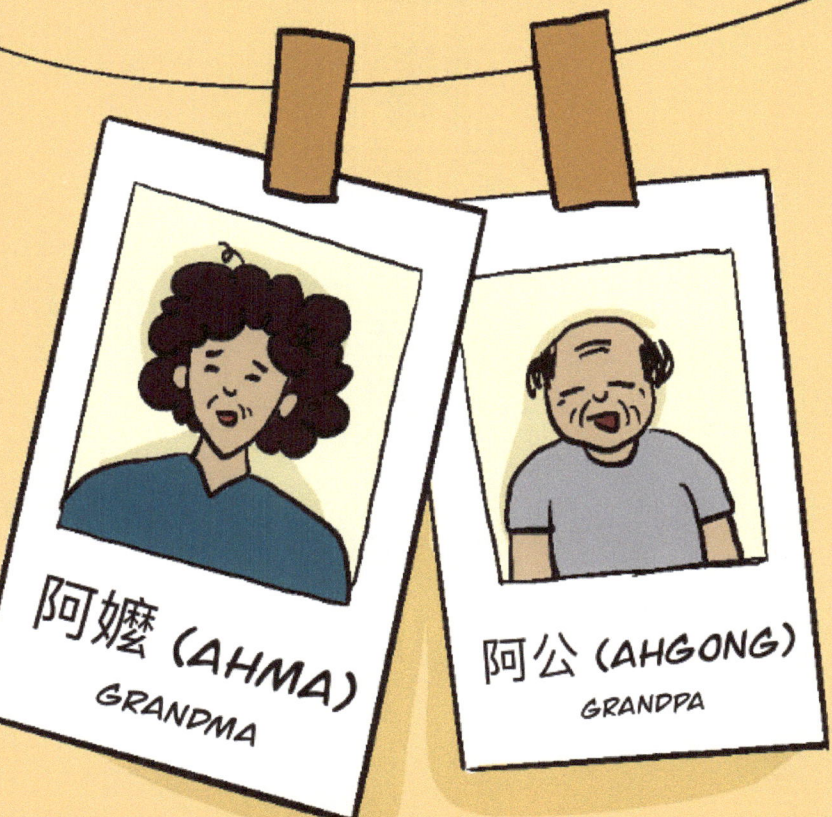

FOR THE FIRST FEW YEARS THAT I LIVED IN TAIWAN, I STAYED IN MY AHMA AND AHGONG'S HOUSE.

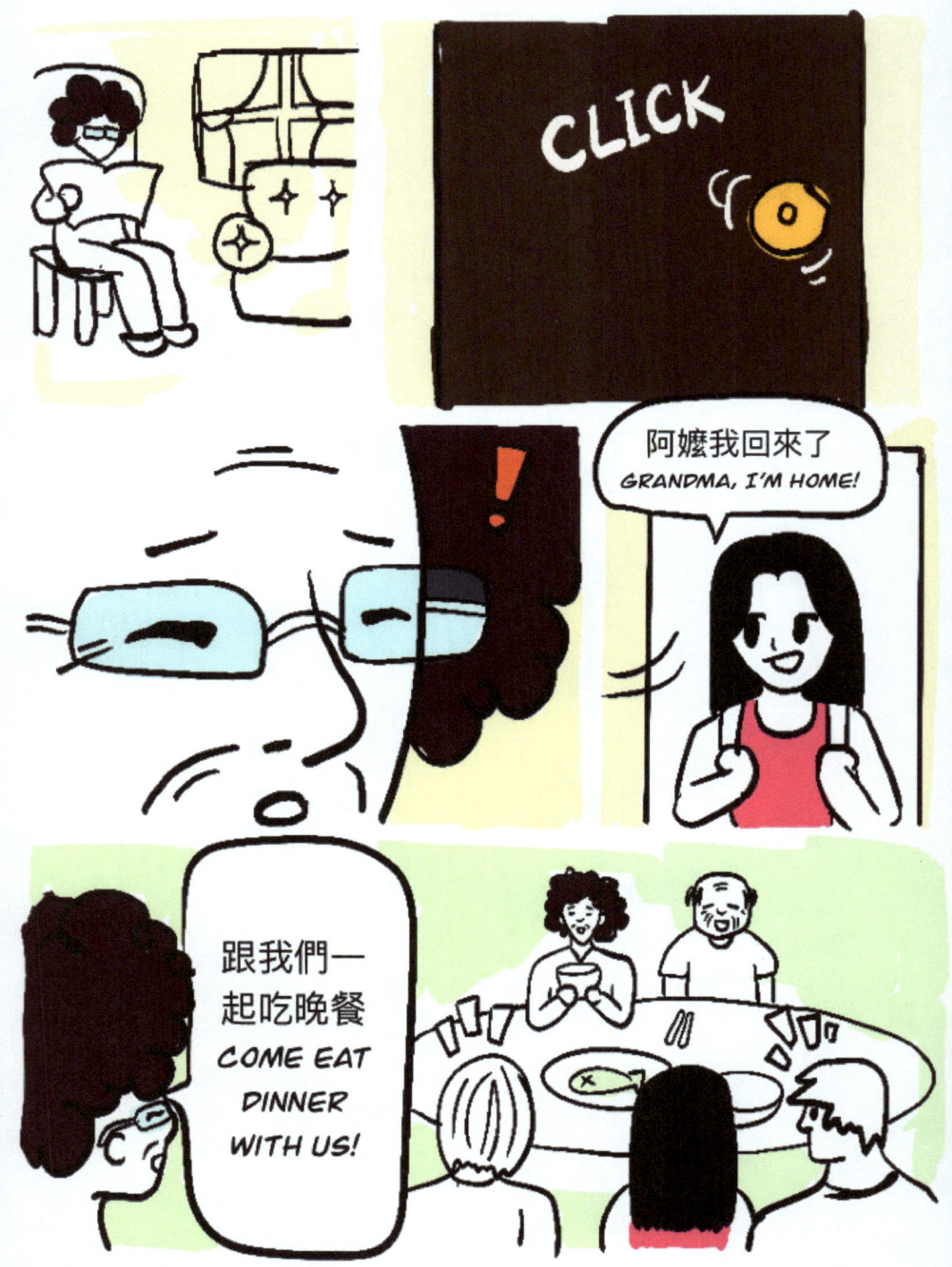

YES, I THINK THAT MANDARIN IS A LOT EASIER THAN CANTONESE.

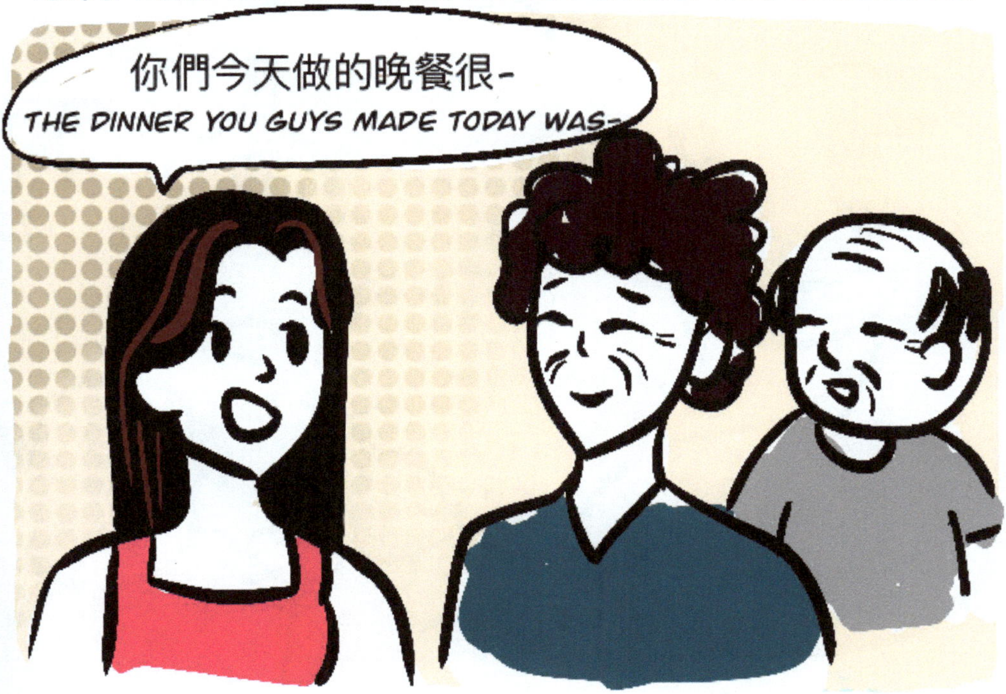

你們今天做的晚餐很-
THE DINNER YOU GUYS MADE TODAY WAS-

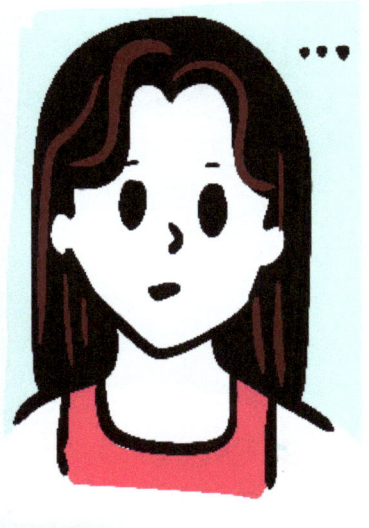
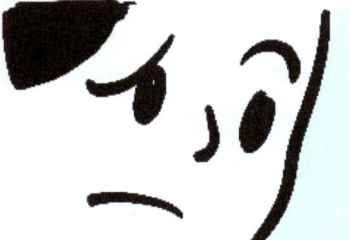

HOWEVER, I COULD NOT TALK TO THEM IN MORE DEPTH BECAUSE OF MY LIMITED MANDARIN VOCABULARY

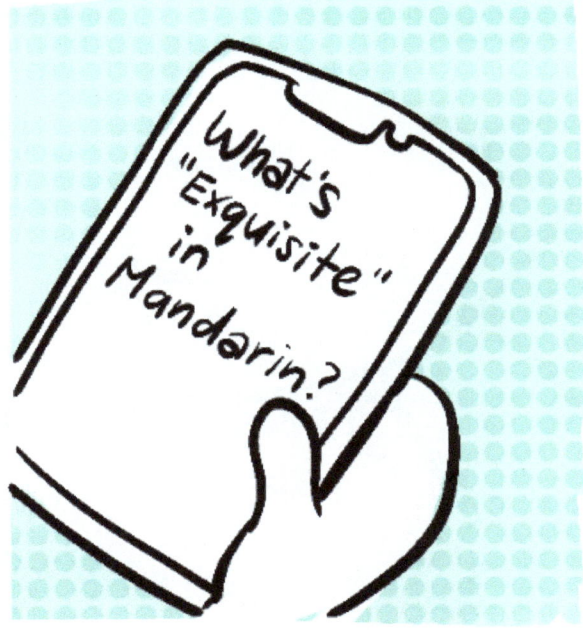

What's "Exquisite" in Mandarin?

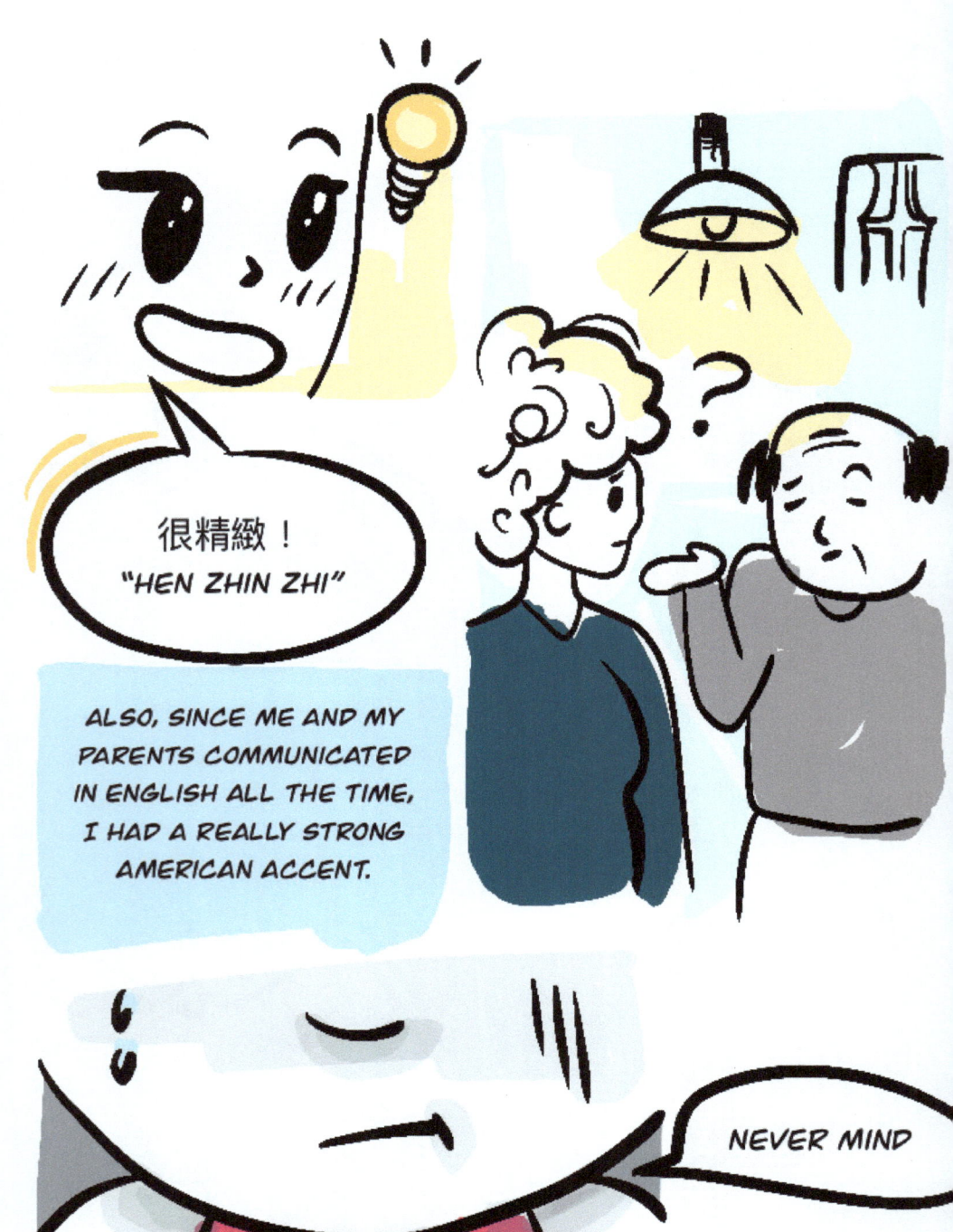

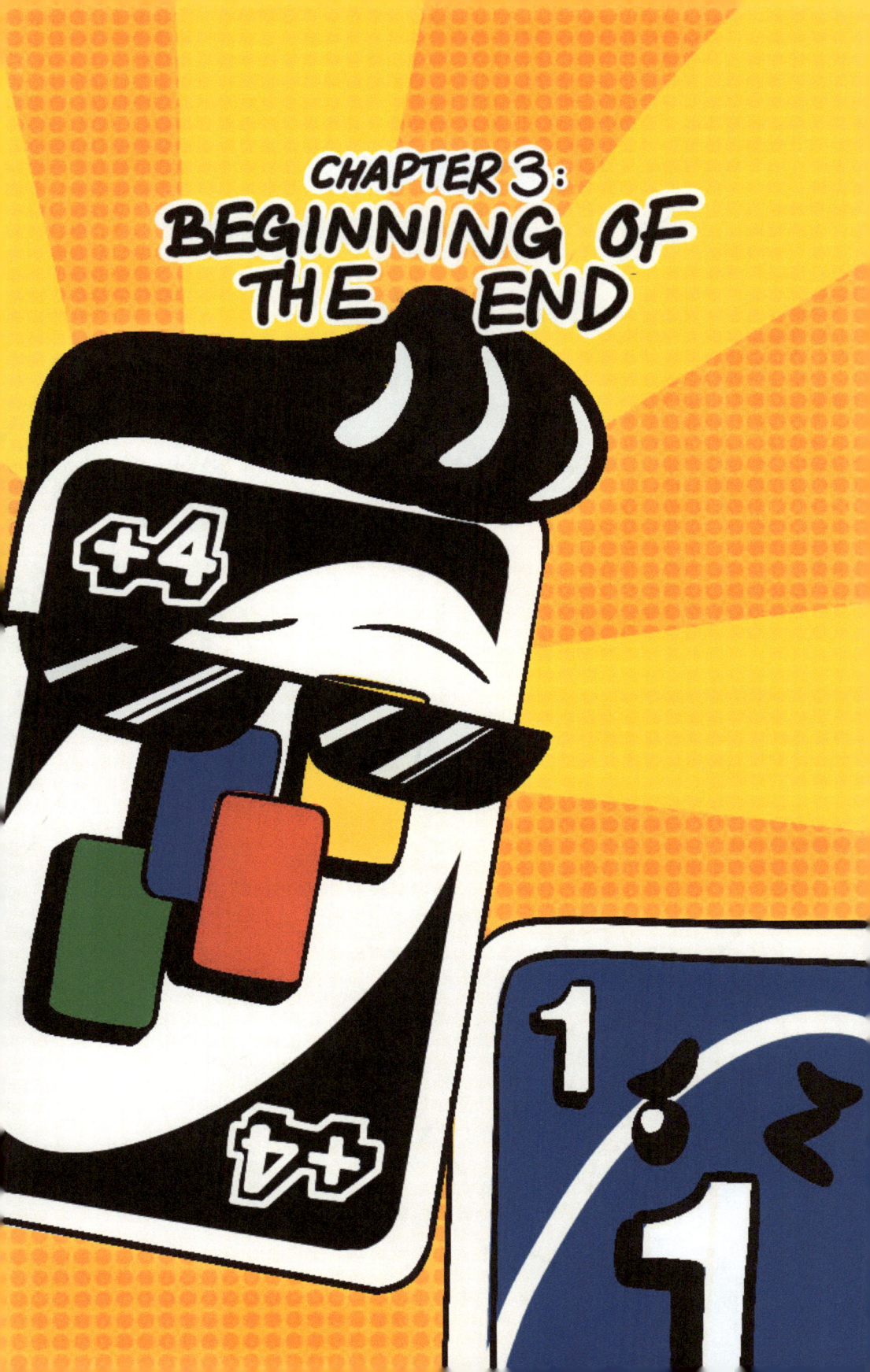

LIFE AT SCHOOL WAS ALSO GREAT. ALTHOUGH MY GRADES WEREN'T ALWAYS THE BEST AT THE TIME, I STILL GOT ALONG WITH MY FRIENDS WELL.

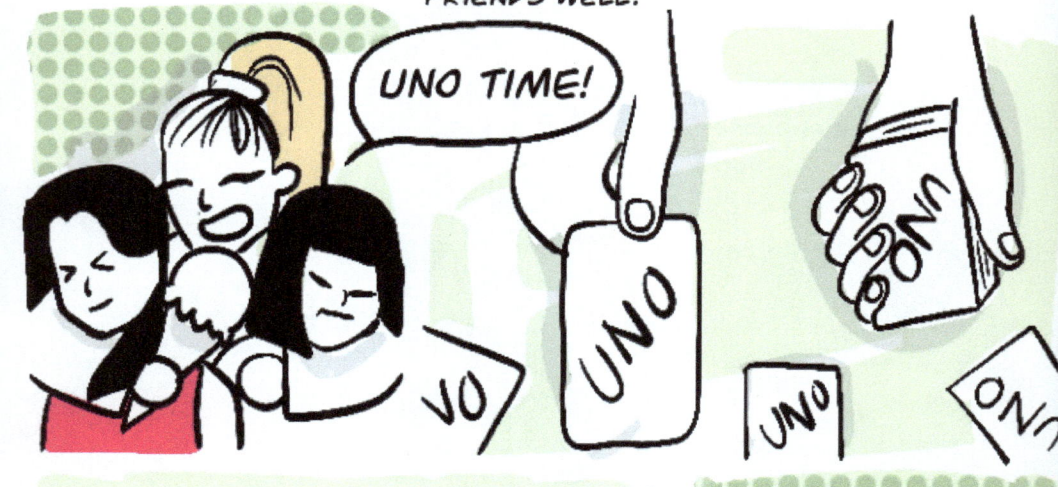

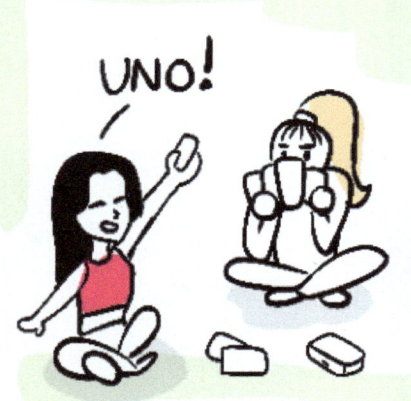

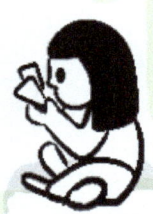

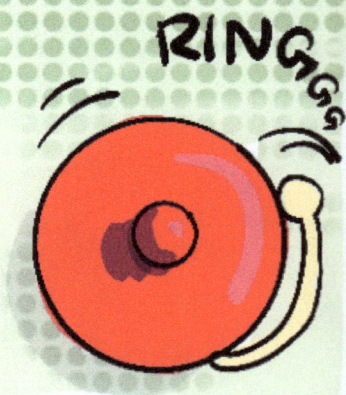

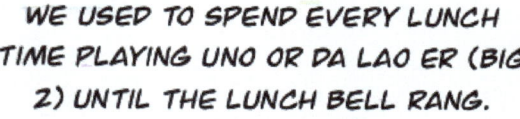

WE USED TO SPEND EVERY LUNCH TIME PLAYING UNO OR DA LAO ER (BIG 2) UNTIL THE LUNCH BELL RANG.

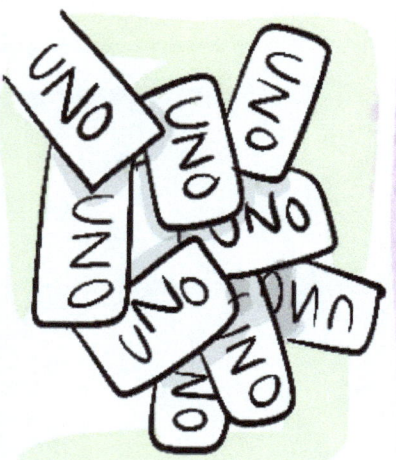

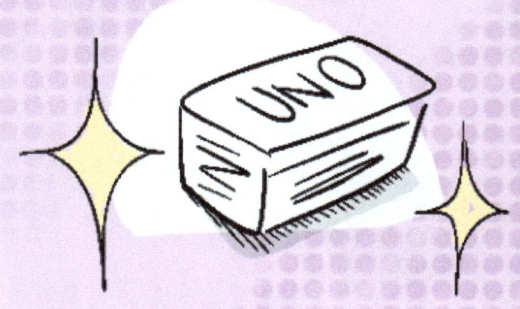

I EVEN GOT INTO THE VARSITY SWIM TEAM IN MY FRESHMAN YEAR AND ANNUALLY SWAM EVER SINCE.

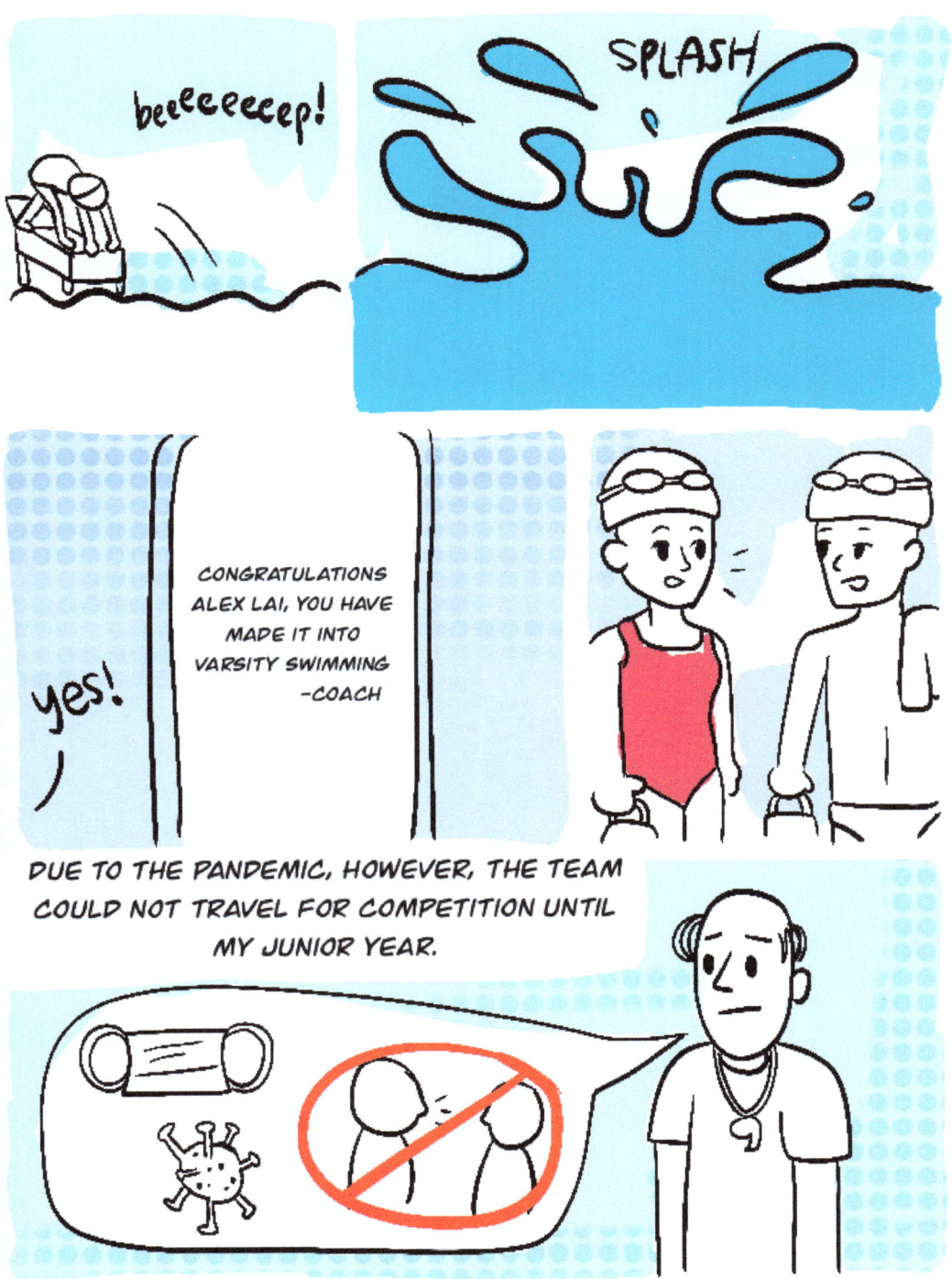

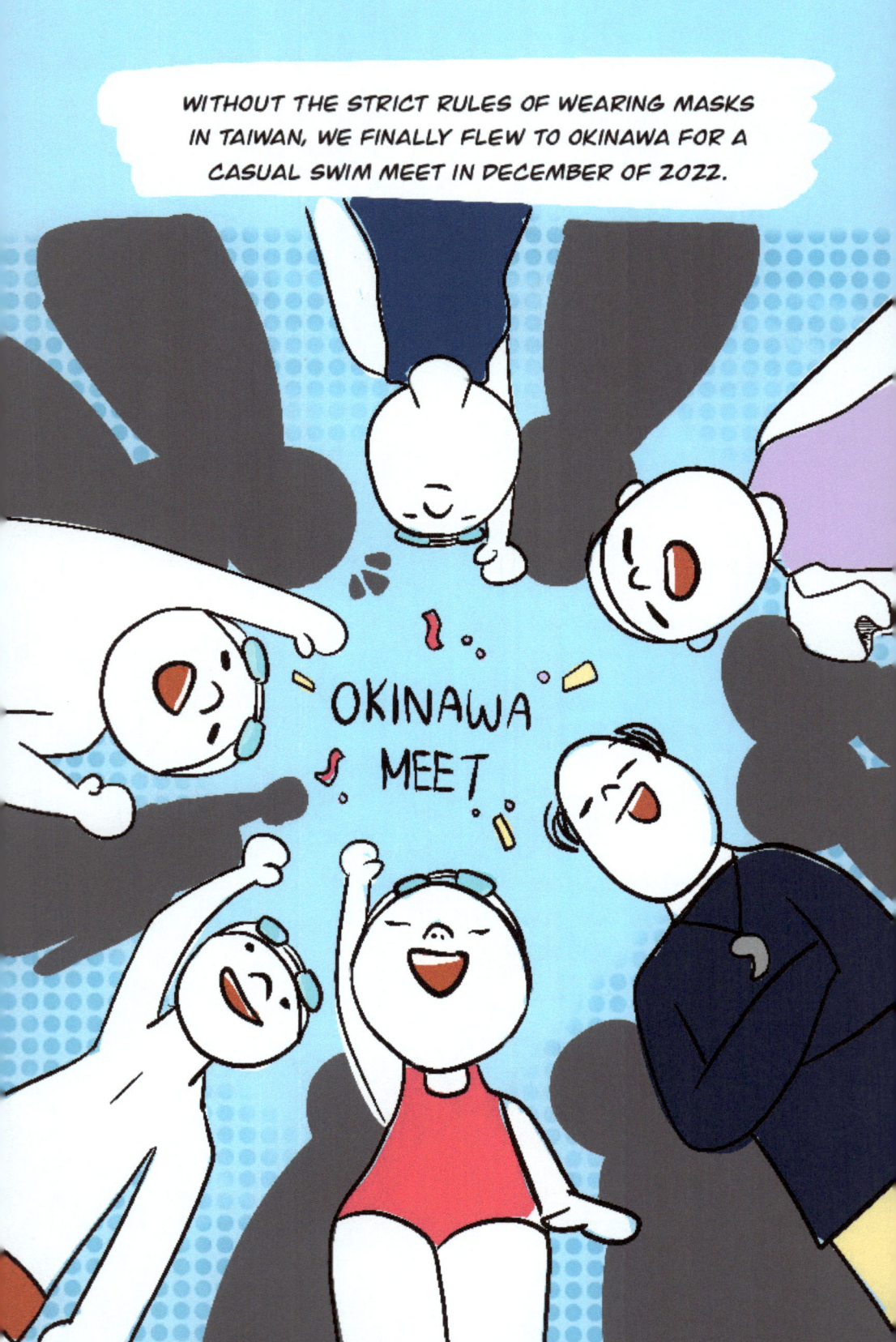

ON THE DAY BEFORE OUR MEET, WE HAD THE OPPORTUNITY TO GO PRACTICE IN THE JAPANESE INTERNATIONAL SCHOOL'S POOL.

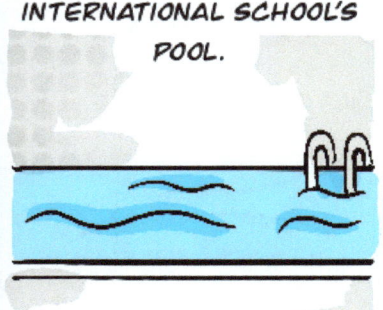

HOWEVER, IT WAS RAINING... AND IT WAS WINTER...

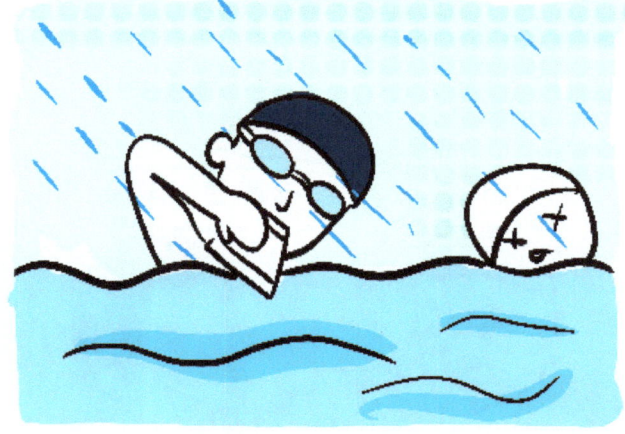

WE SWAM IN WHAT I CAN ONLY DESCRIBE AS AN ICE BATH.

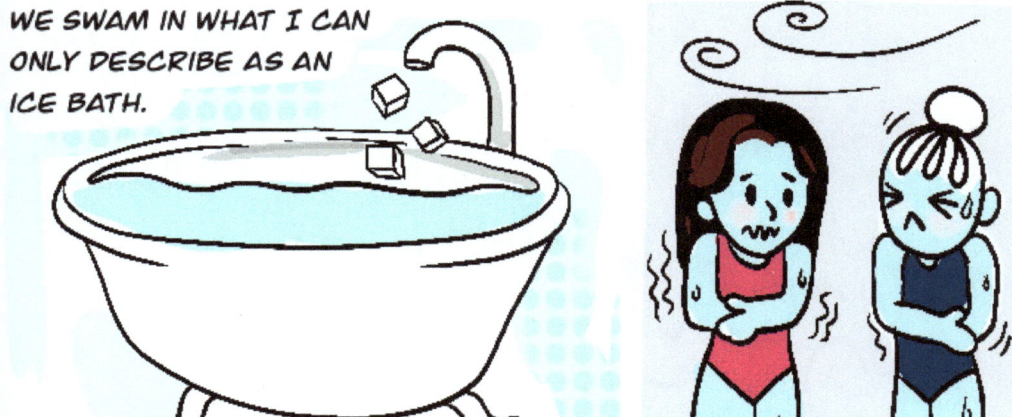

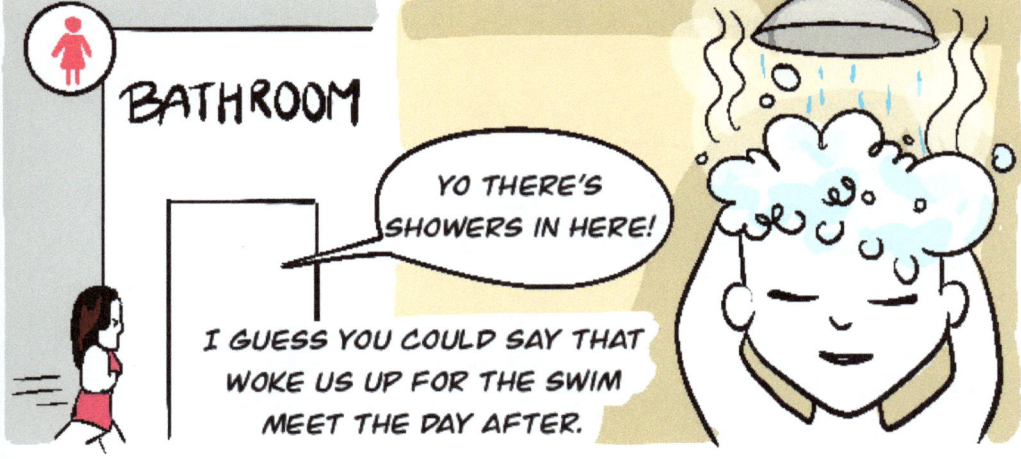

BATHROOM

YO THERE'S SHOWERS IN HERE!

I GUESS YOU COULD SAY THAT WOKE US UP FOR THE SWIM MEET THE DAY AFTER.

ON THE DAY OF THE SWIM MEET. EVERYONE
ON THE TEAM BEAT AT LEAST ONE
PERSONAL BEST TIME.

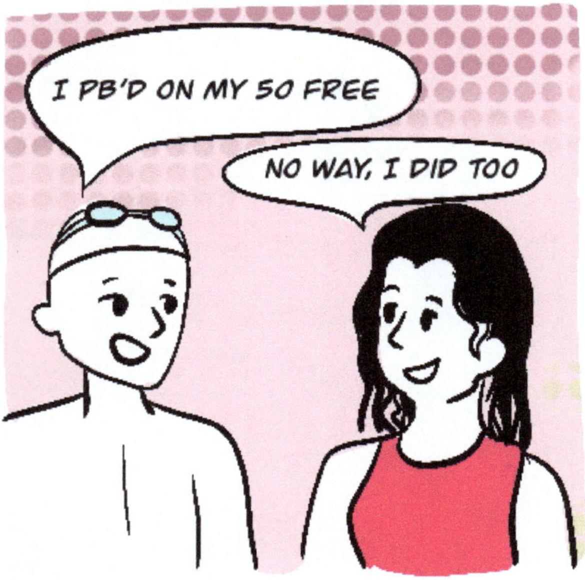

I PB'D ON MY 50 FREE

NO WAY, I DID TOO

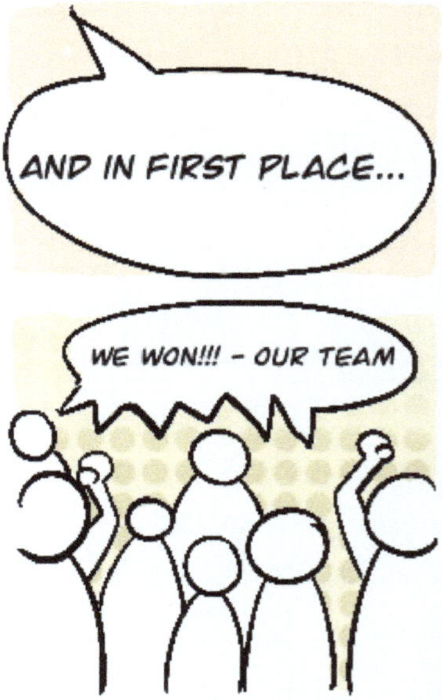

AND IN FIRST PLACE...

WE WON!!! – OUR TEAM

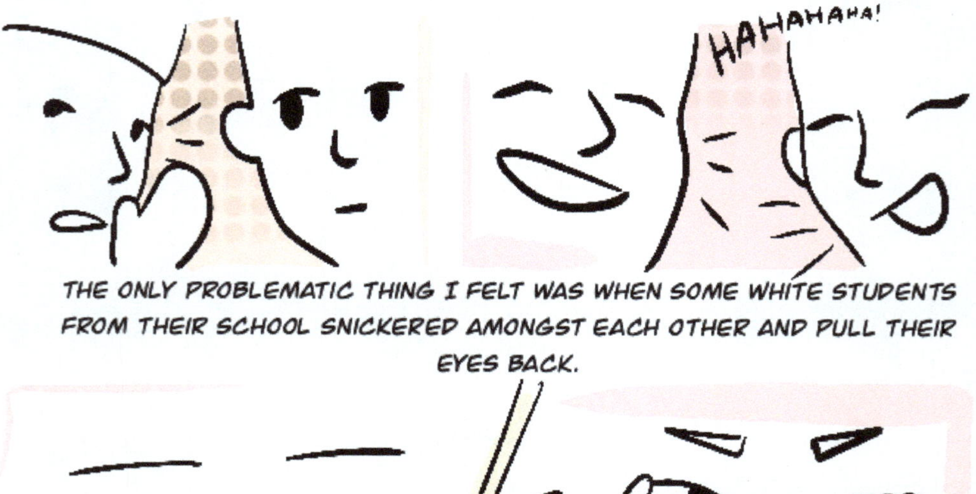

HAHAHAHA!

THE ONLY PROBLEMATIC THING I FELT WAS WHEN SOME WHITE STUDENTS
FROM THEIR SCHOOL SNICKERED AMONGST EACH OTHER AND PULL THEIR
EYES BACK.

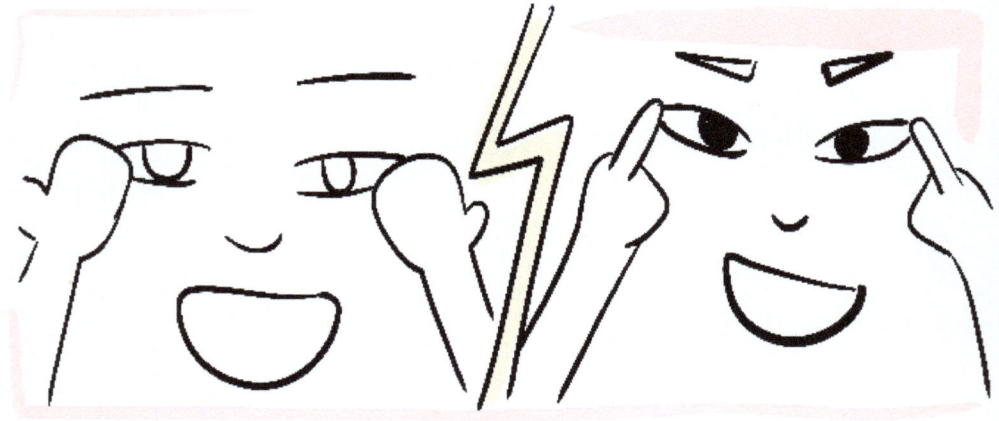

DURING THE EVENTS, SWIMMERS HAD TO STAND IN A LINE ACCORDING TO WHICH LANE WE WOULD BE SWIMMING IN. IF YOU WERE IN LANE 6, YOU WOULD BE 6TH IN LINE.

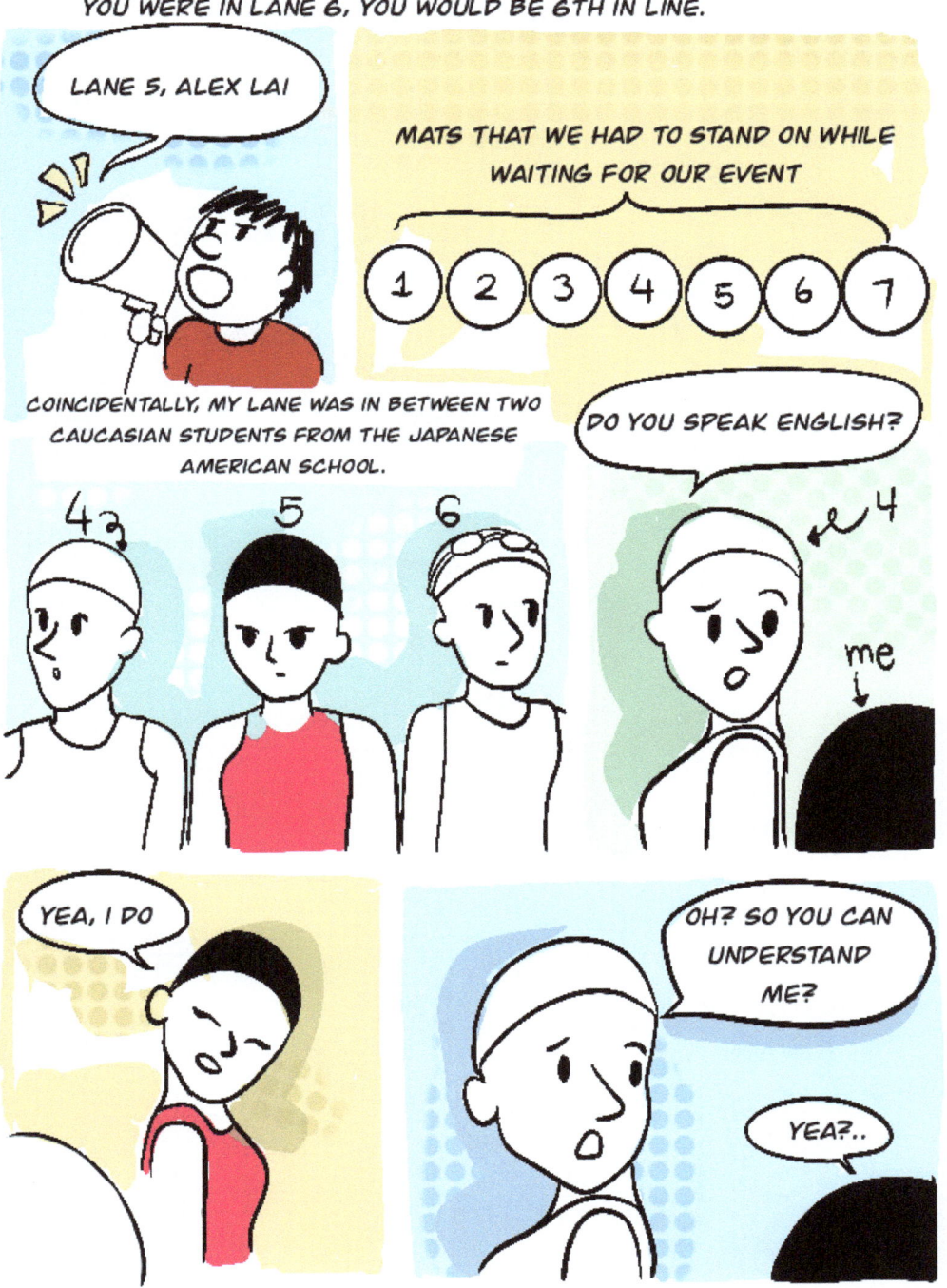

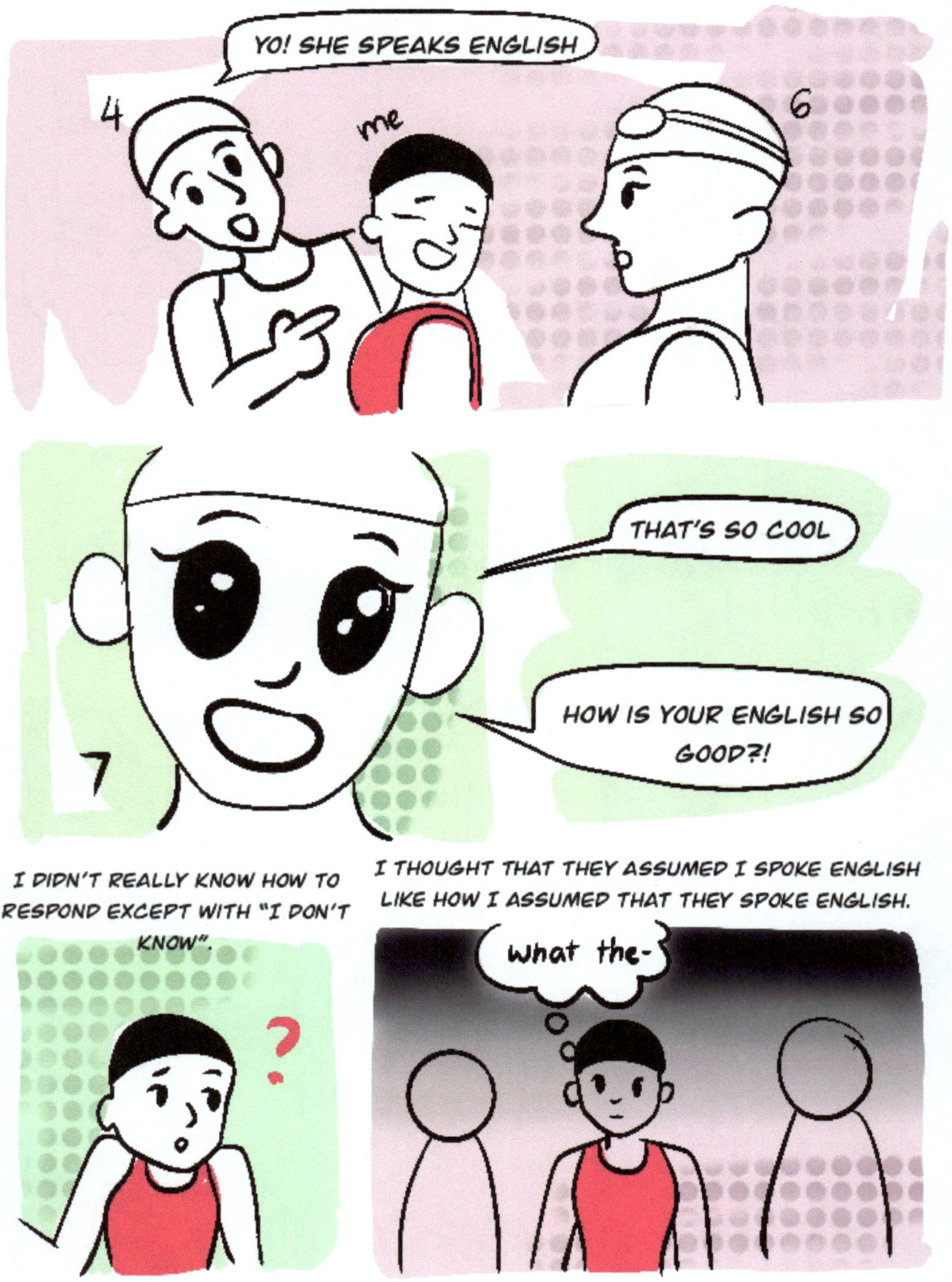

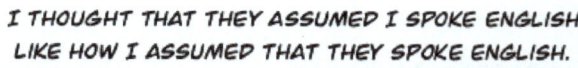

I DIDN'T REALLY KNOW HOW TO RESPOND EXCEPT WITH "I DON'T KNOW".

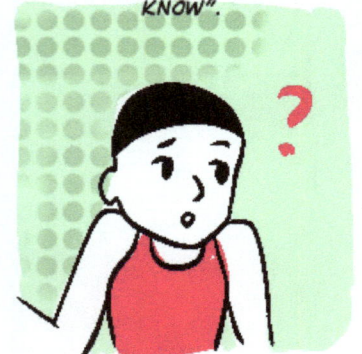
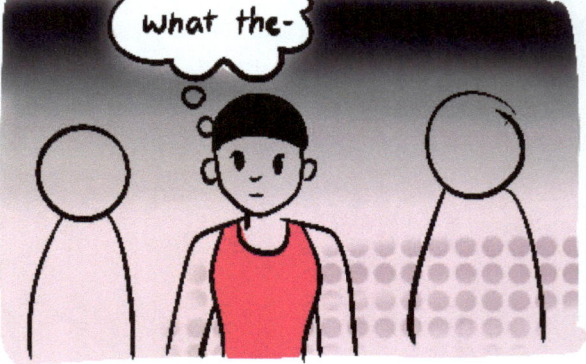

CHAPTER 4: COMING BACK

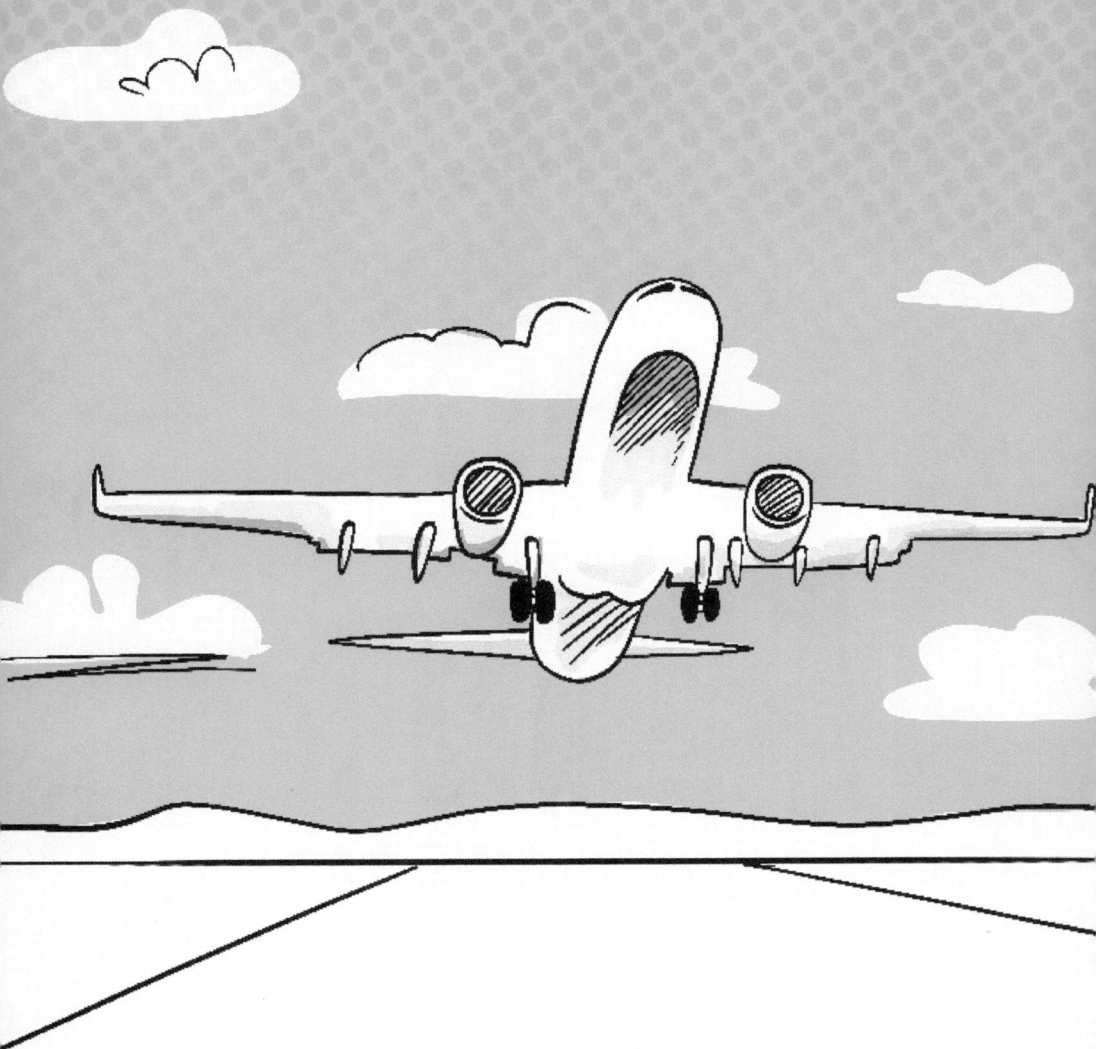

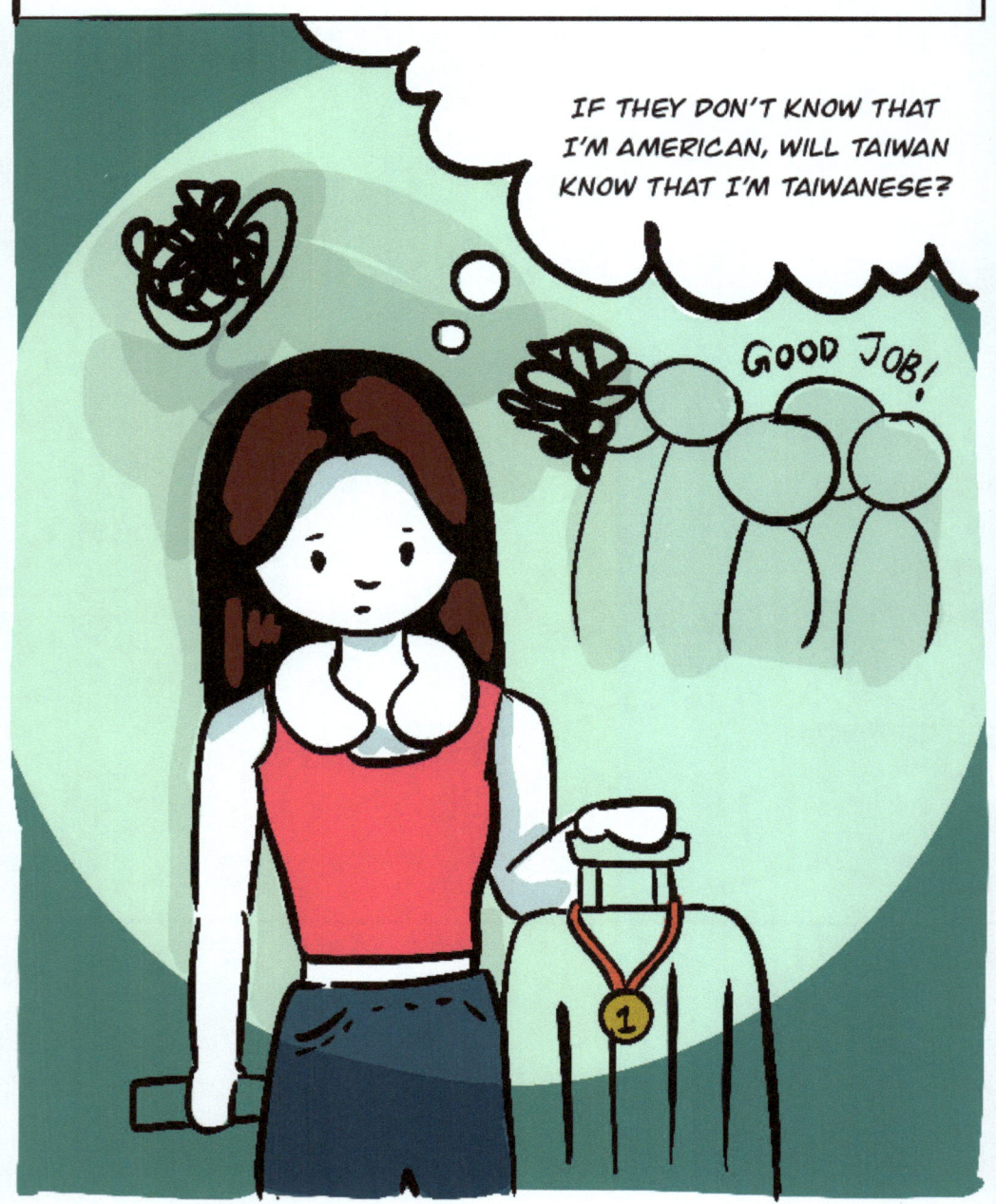

I NOTICED THAT I ENCOUNTERED MORE AND MORE PEOPLE WHO MISUNDERSTOOD WHERE I CAME FROM BECAUSE OF MY ACCENT

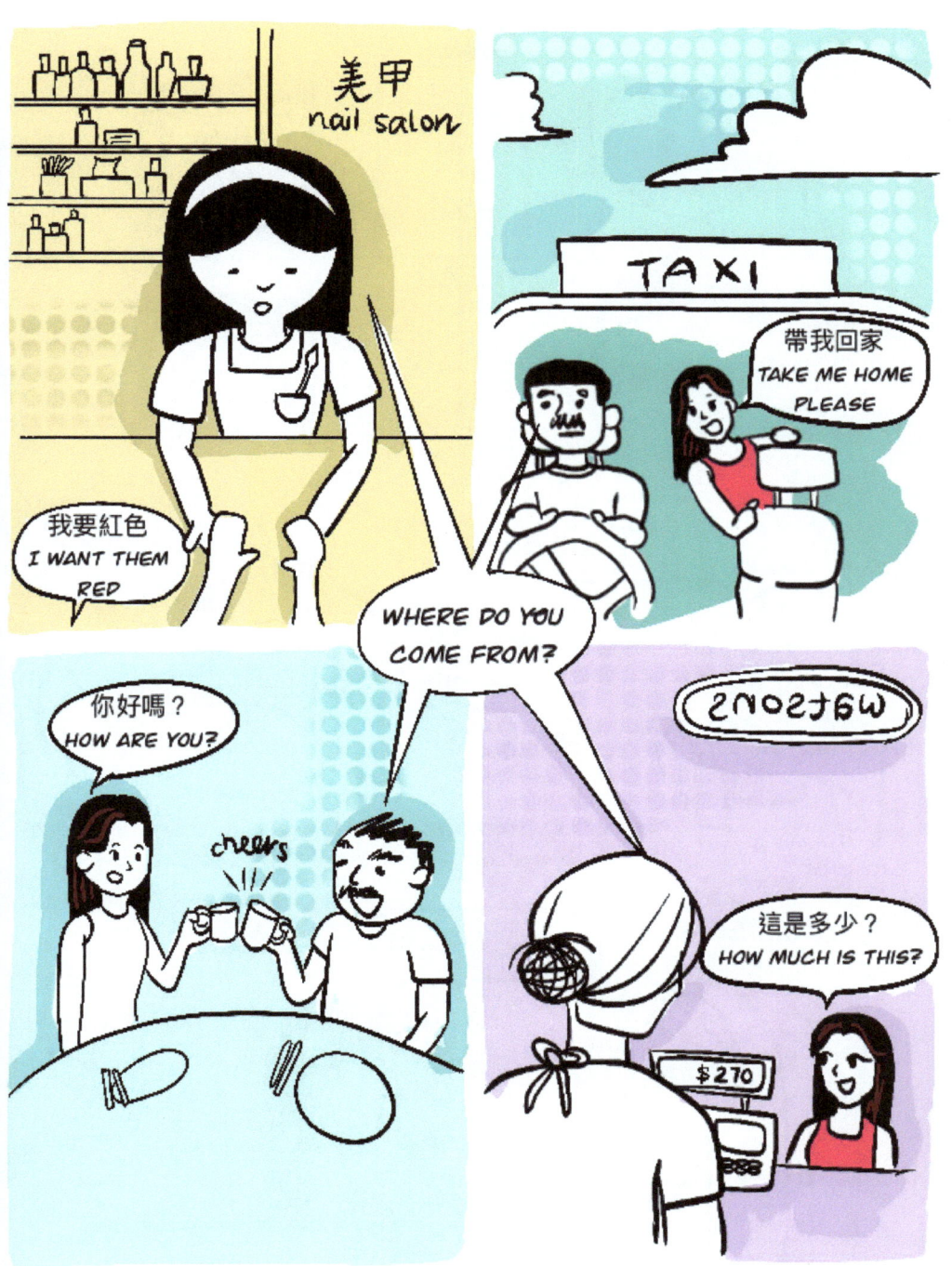

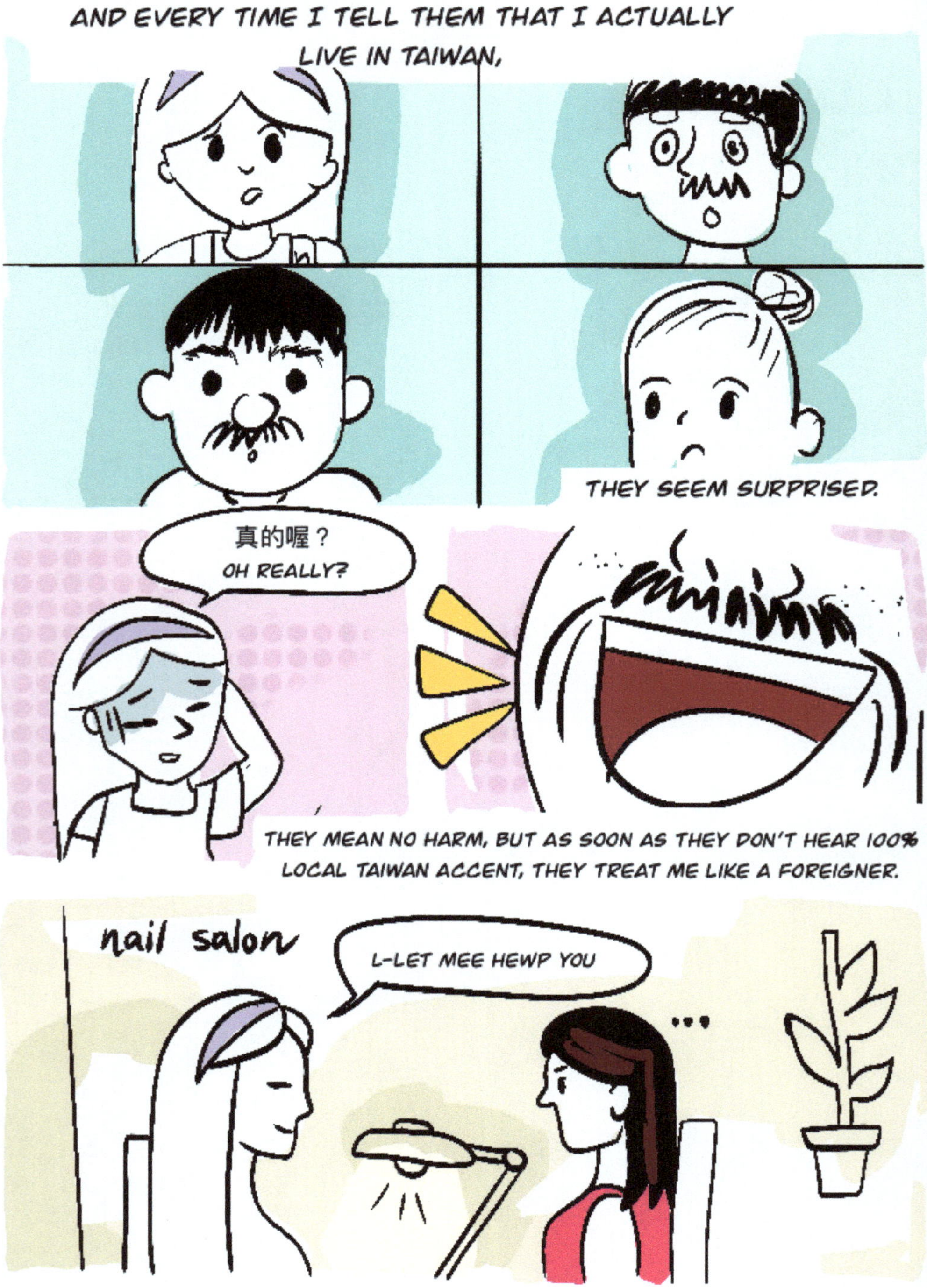

AND EVERY TIME I TELL THEM THAT I ACTUALLY
LIVE IN TAIWAN,

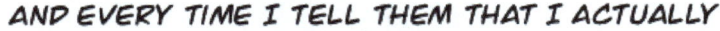

THEY SEEM SURPRISED.

真的喔？
OH REALLY?

THEY MEAN NO HARM, BUT AS SOON AS THEY DON'T HEAR 100%
LOCAL TAIWAN ACCENT, THEY TREAT ME LIKE A FOREIGNER.

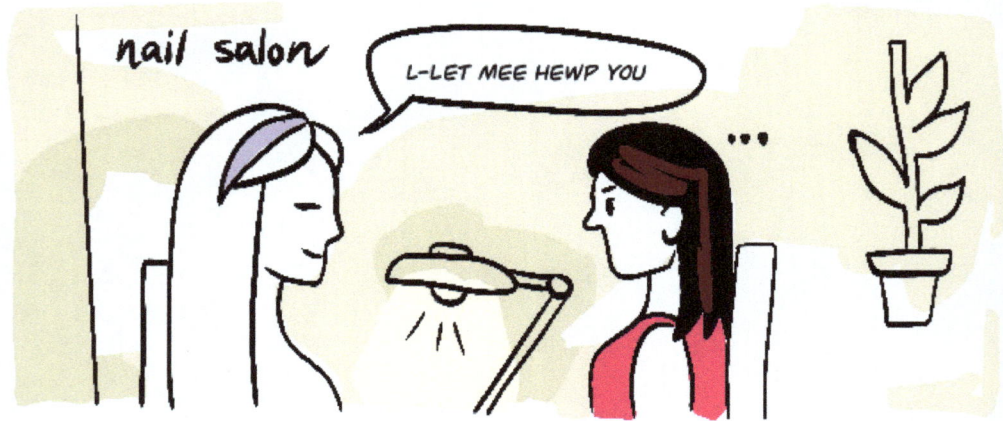

nail salon

L-LET MEE HEWP YOU

...

CHAPTER 5: ADDING FUEL

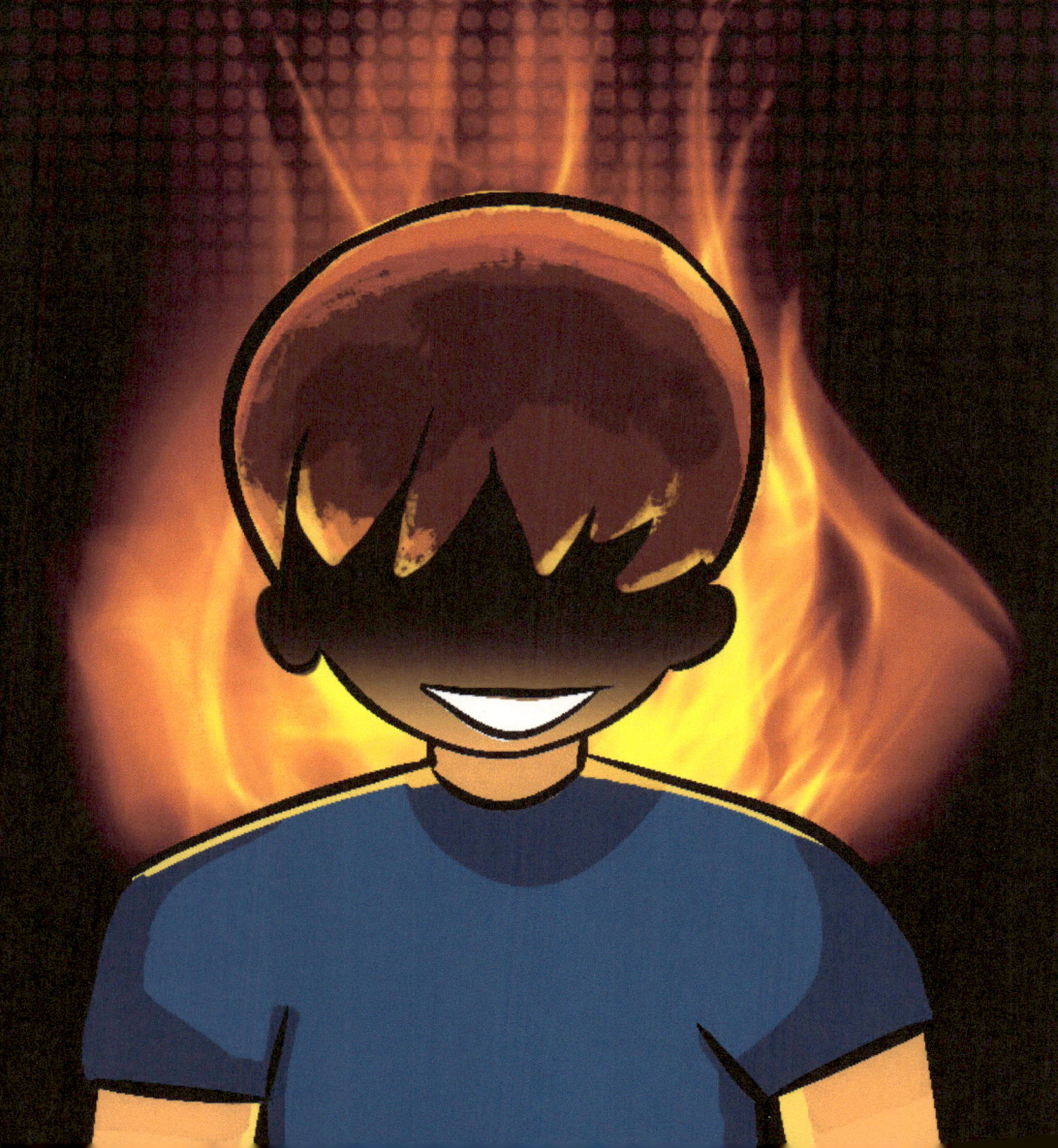

IN THE SUMMER OF 2023, I WENT TO SUMMER SCHOOL AT A UNIVERSITY IN LA. THE CULTURE SHOCK I EXPERIENCE WAS DRASTIC.

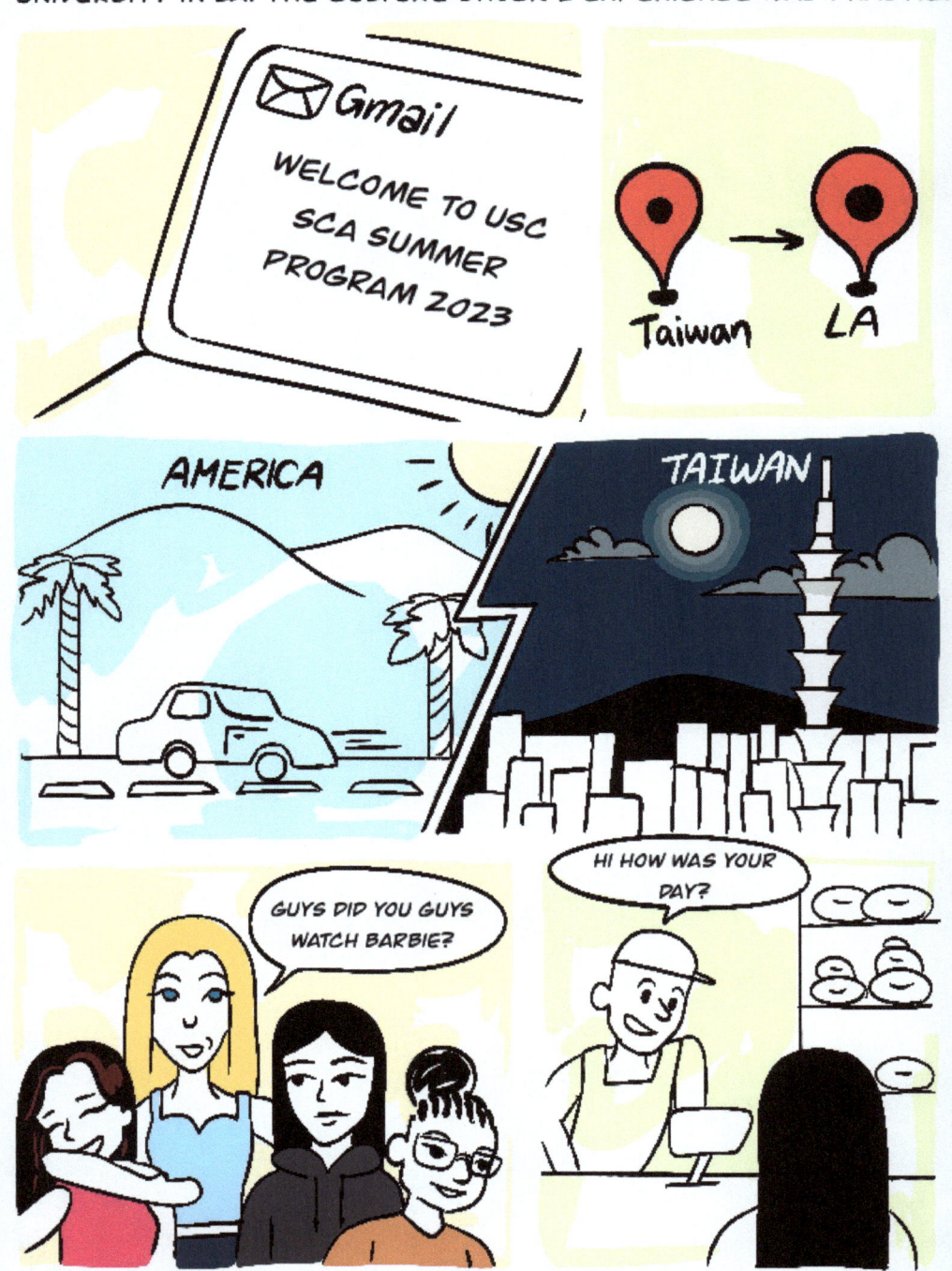

WITH THIS, I NOTICED THAT AMERICANS OFTEN WANTED TO KNOW ABOUT MY PERSONAL LIFE; WHEREAS EVERYBODY IN TAIWAN WAS A LOT MORE RESERVED.

SOMETIMES, HOWEVER, I ALSO EXPERIENCED CULTURE SHOCK DUE TO HOW BLUNT AND UNCENSORED SOME PEOPLE WERE IN AMERICA.

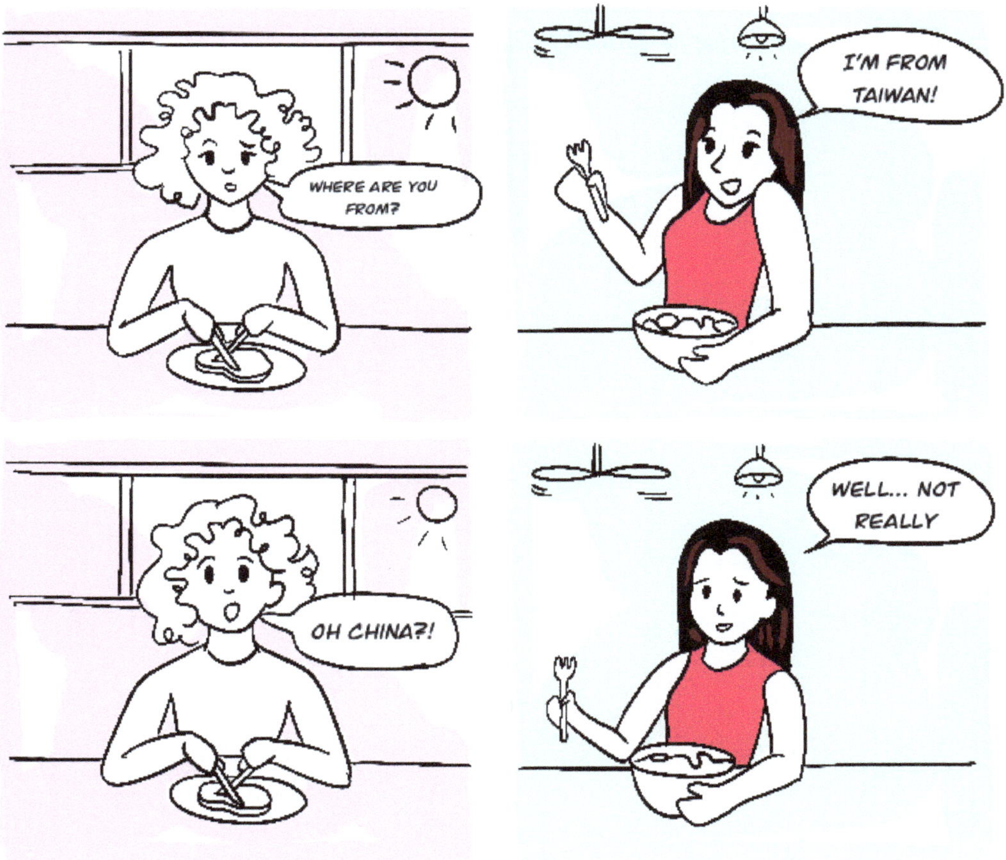

WHERE ARE YOU FROM?

I'M FROM TAIWAN!

OH CHINA?!

WELL... NOT REALLY

I DON'T HAVE THE GUTS TO TELL THEM ALL THE POLITICAL CONVERSATIONS AND CONTROVERSIES SURROUNDING THAT TOPIC...

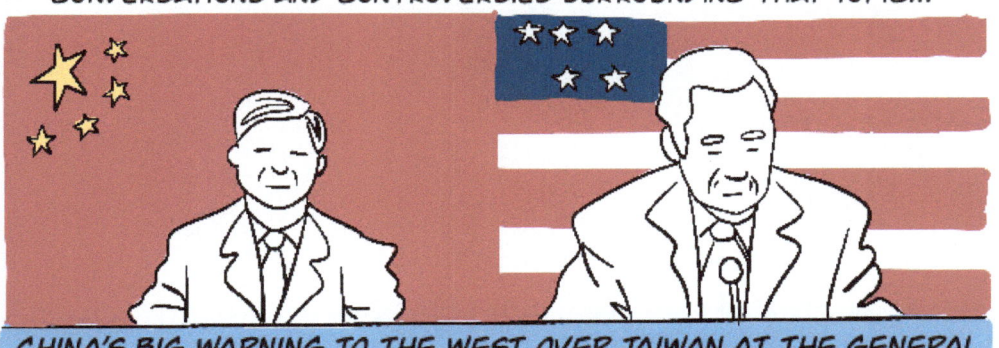

CHINA'S BIG WARNING TO THE WEST OVER TAIWAN AT THE GENERAL ASSEMBLY

BESIDES BEING MIS-IDENTIFIED, I ALSO FACED SOME OTHER CONTROVERSIES REGARDING WHERE I CAME FROM.

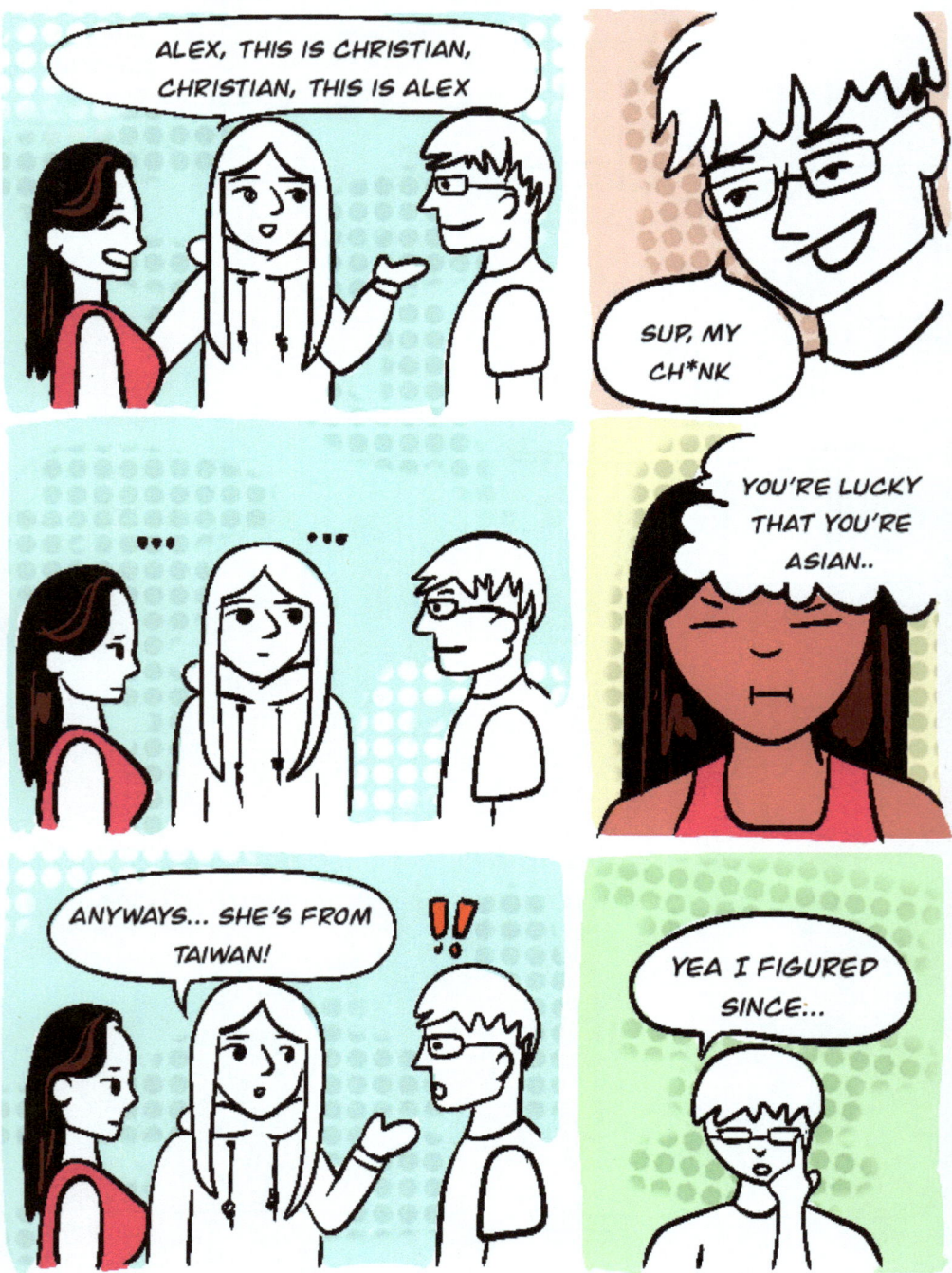

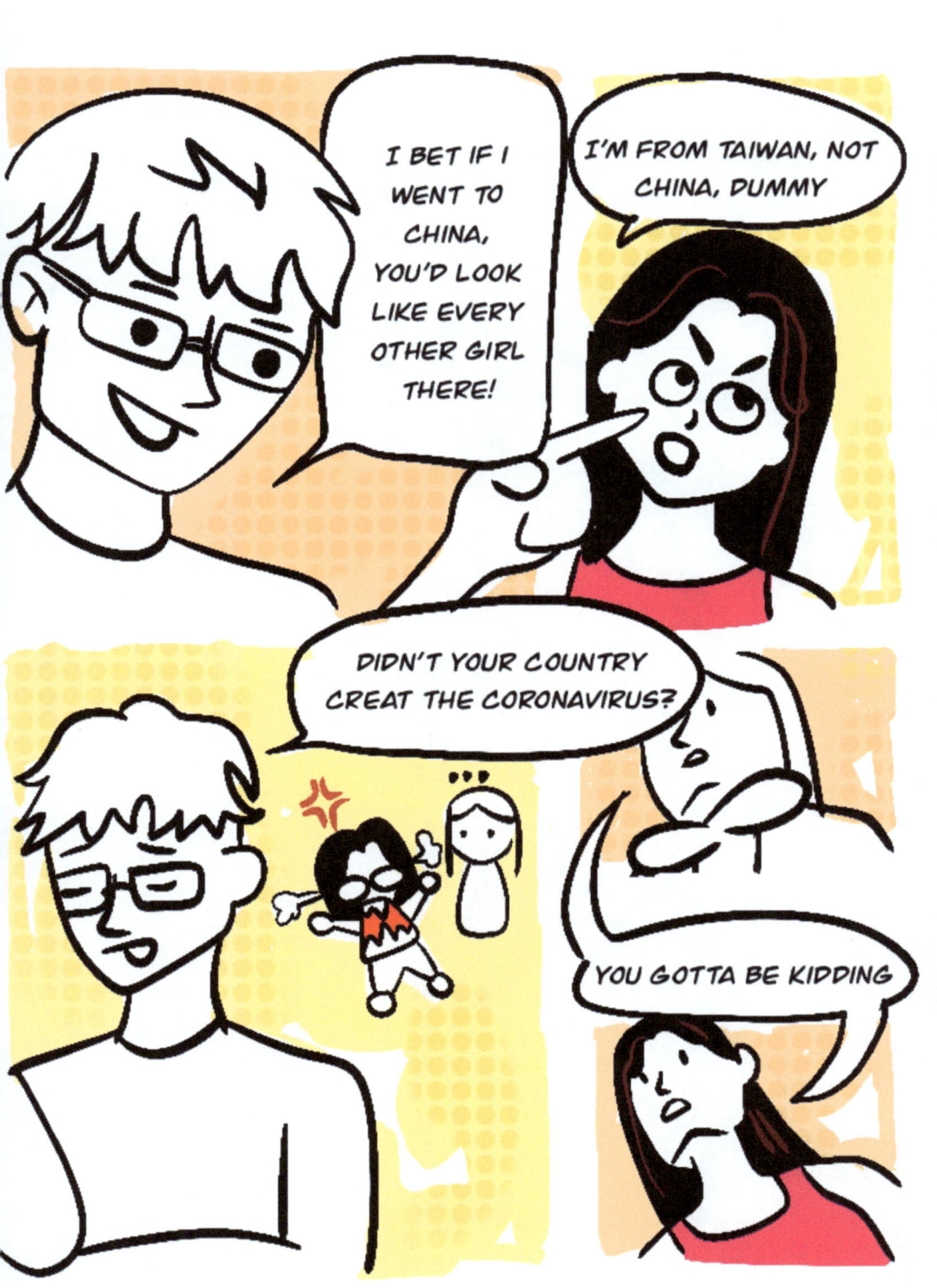

I DIDN'T KNOW WHAT CHRISTIAN'S GOAL WAS

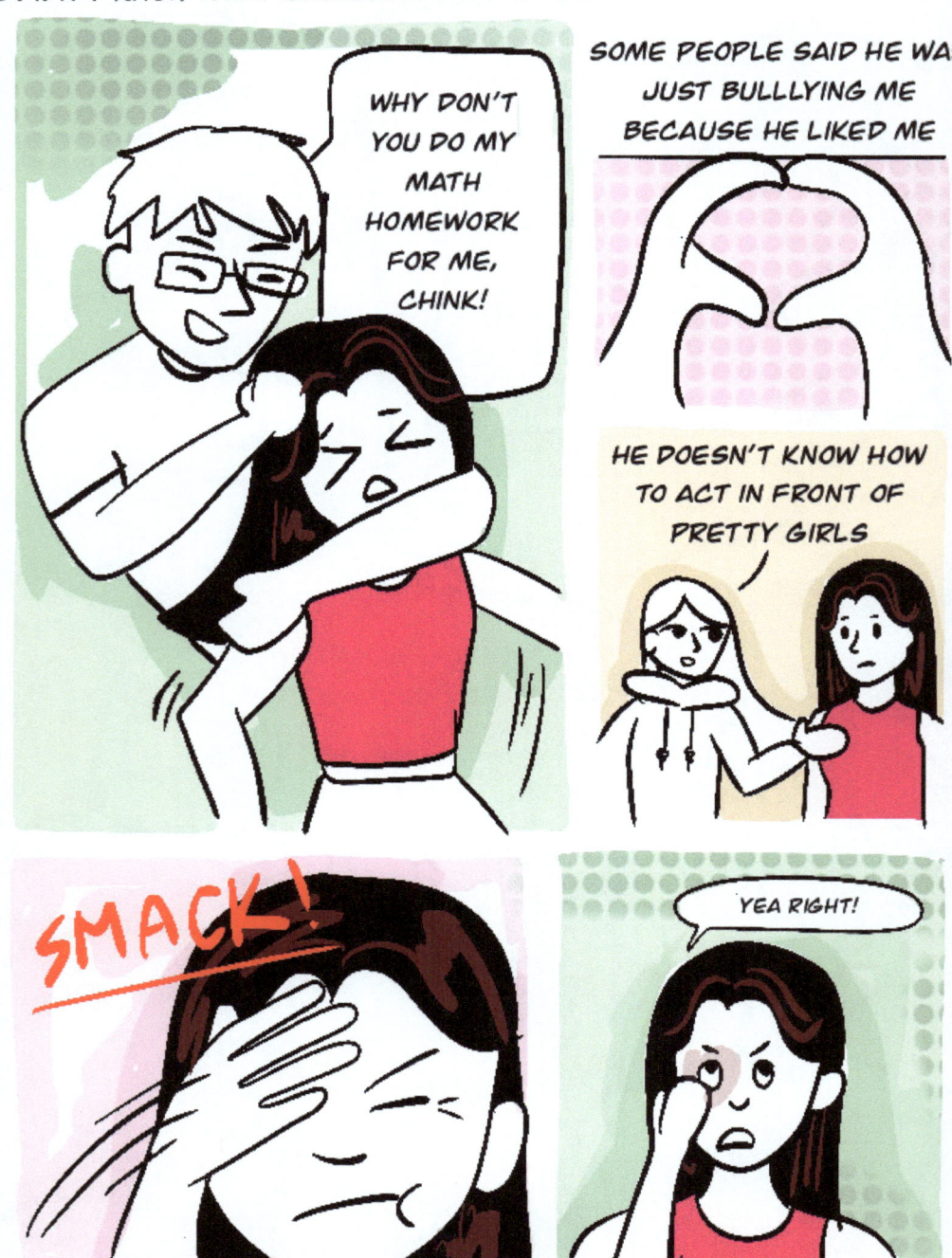

I DOUBT IT THOUGH. I MEAN, WHO WOULD DO THIS?

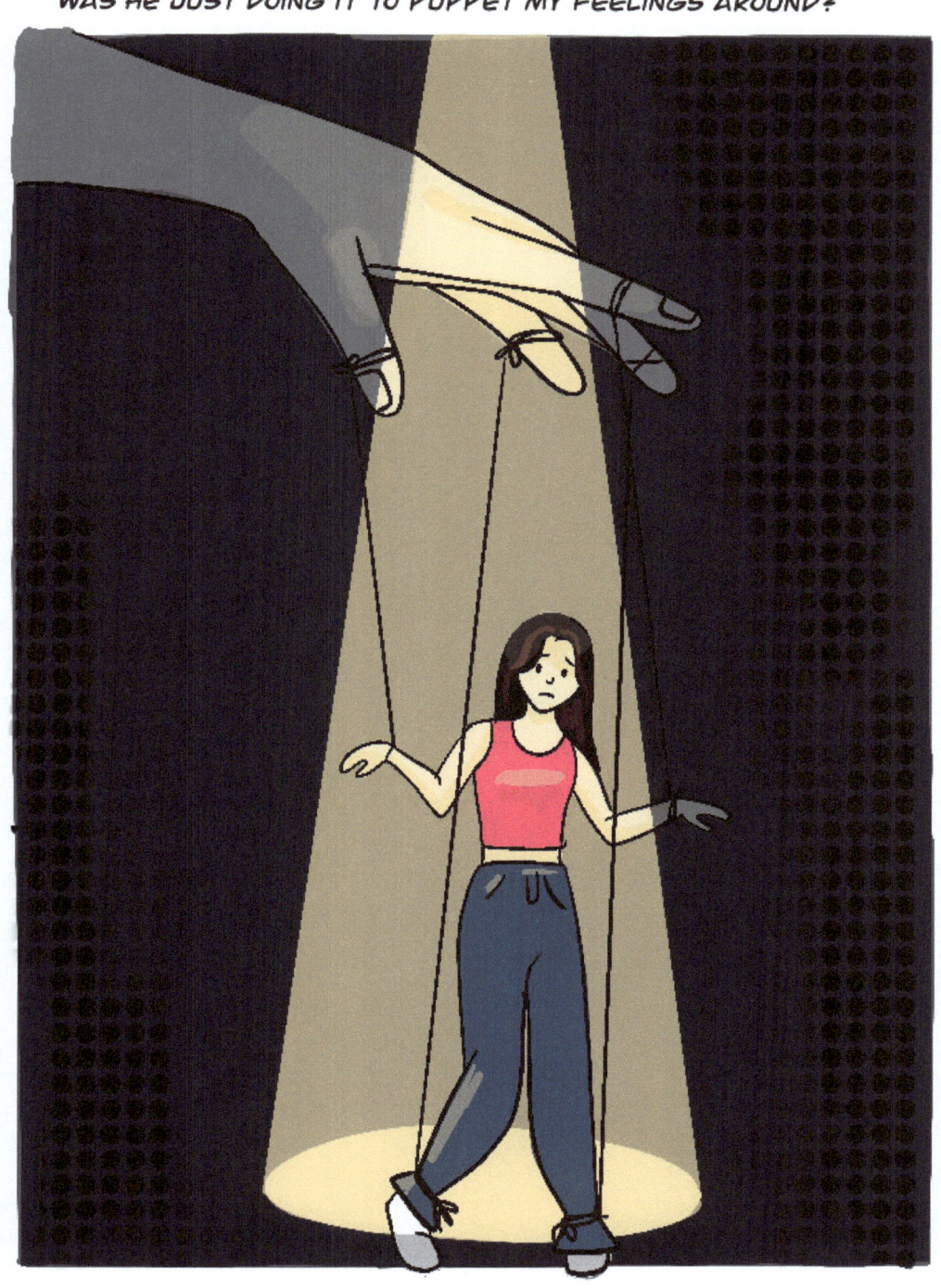

TYPICALLY, I WOULD LAUGH AT OTHER SILLY AND STEREOTYPICAL ASIAN JOKES. YET, THIS "JOKE" DID NOT SEEM FUNNY TO ME. I NEVER ASKED TO BE THE CAUSE OF A PANDEMIC.

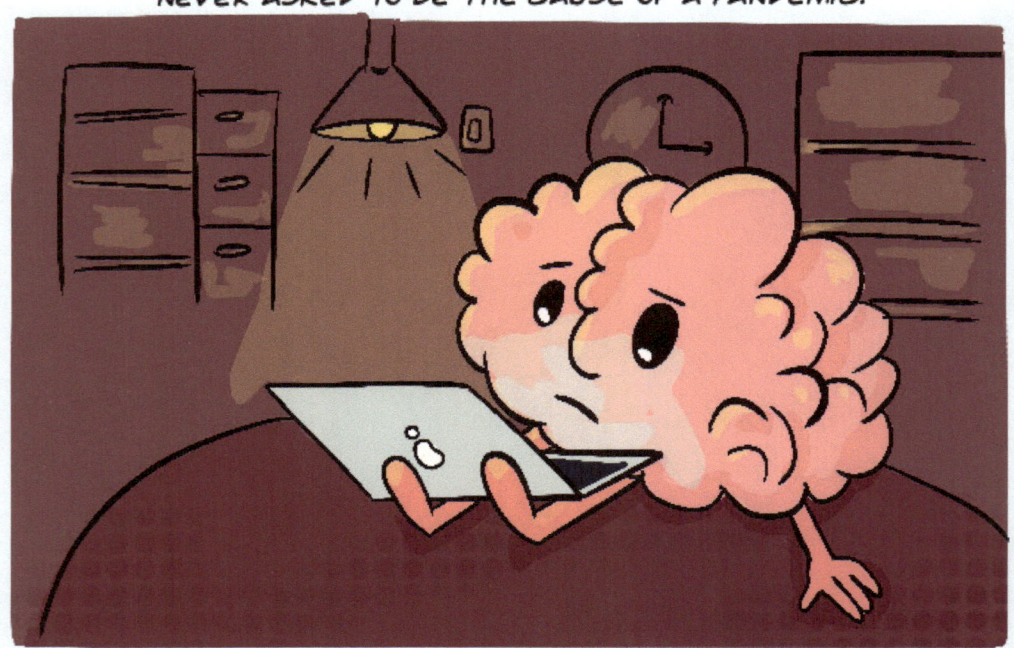

IN MY MIND, THESE KINDS OF OCCURRENCES ONLY SEEMED TO APPEAR IN MOVIES OR TV, AND DID NOT SEEM VERY REALISTIC BECAUSE IT NEVER HAPPENED TO ME

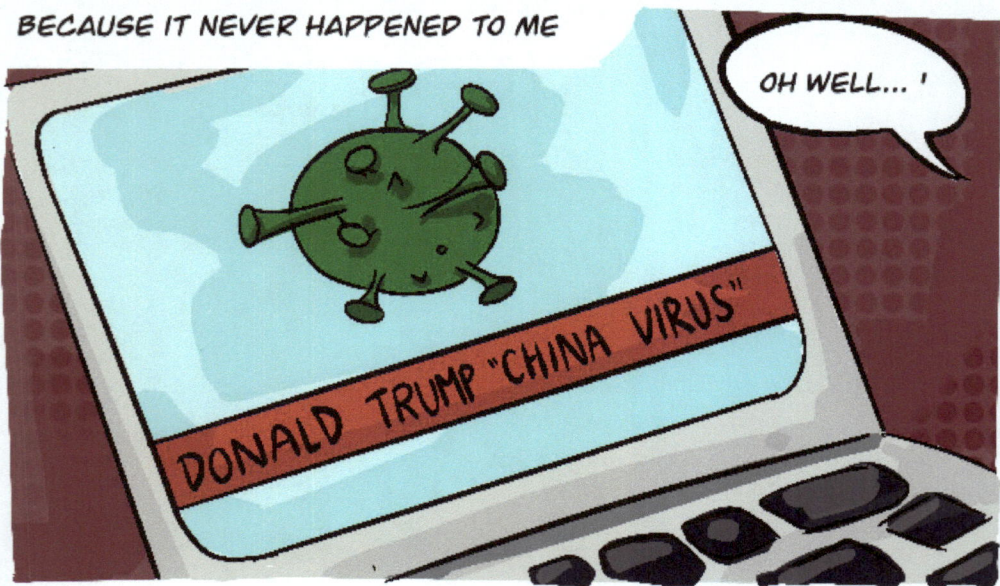

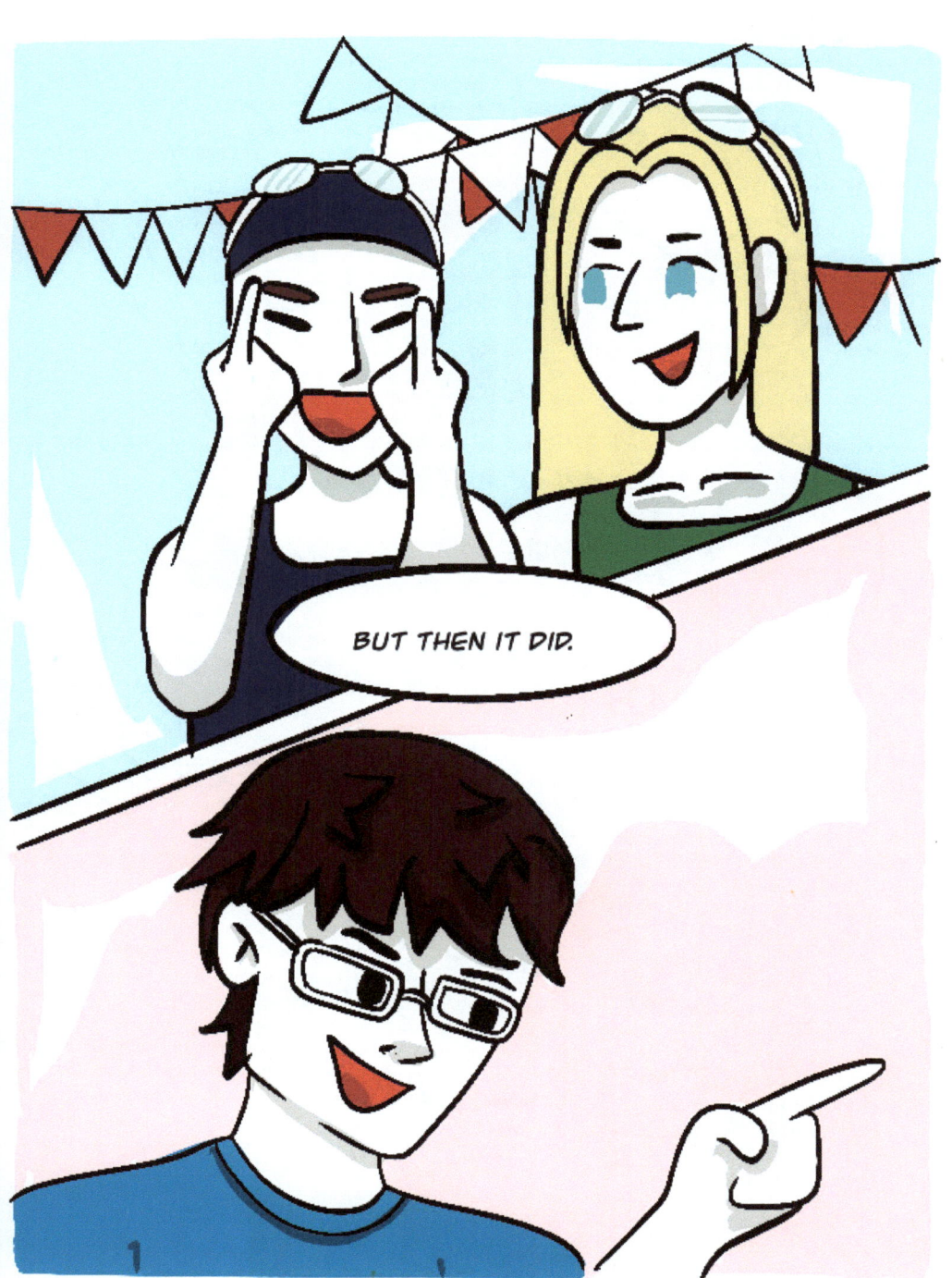

LOOKING BACK, I SHOULD HAVE SCOLDED THEM ABOUT THE INSENSITIVE COMMENTS AND NATURE BEHIND THEIR ACTIONS.

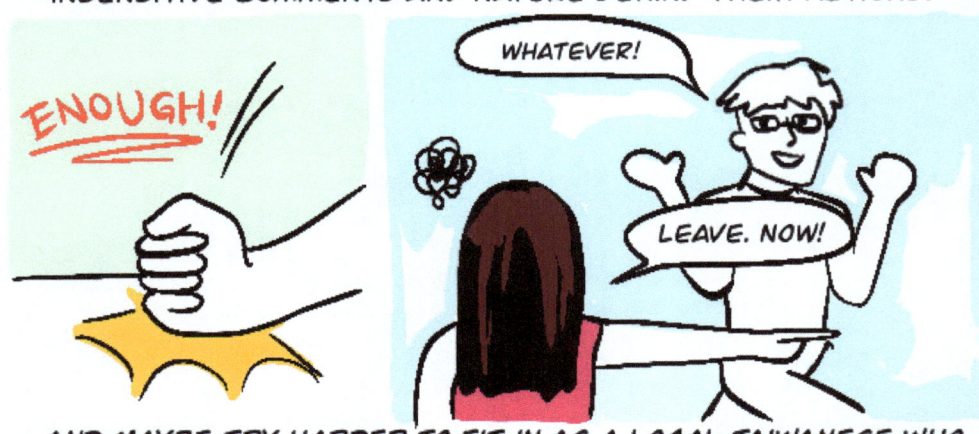

AND MAYBE TRY HARDER TO FIT IN AS A LOCAL TAIWANESE WHO COULD SPEAK FLUENT MANDARIN

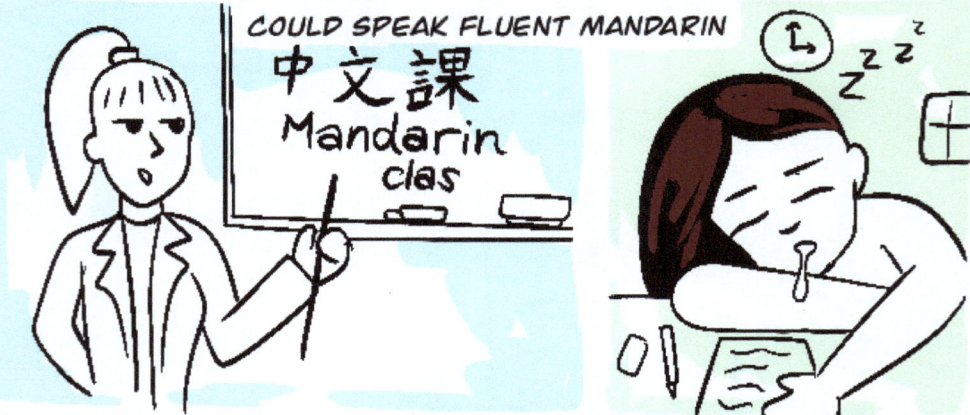

YET, I DON'T THINK ANY AMOUNT OF WORDS WOULD HAVE BEEN IMPACTFUL ENOUGH.

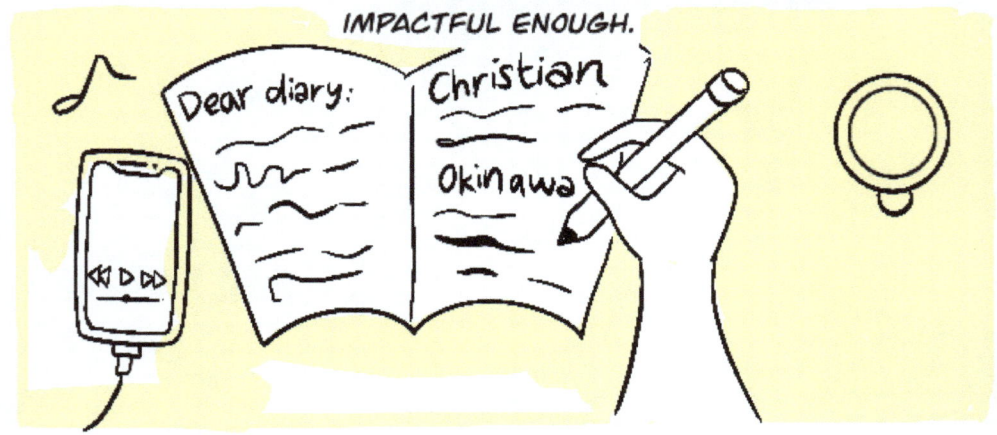

AS A SOLUTION, INSTEAD OF WORRYING ABOUT WHAT
THEY SAID, I ACCEPTED THAT NOT EVERYONE IS GOING
TO BE IN FAVOR OF ME.

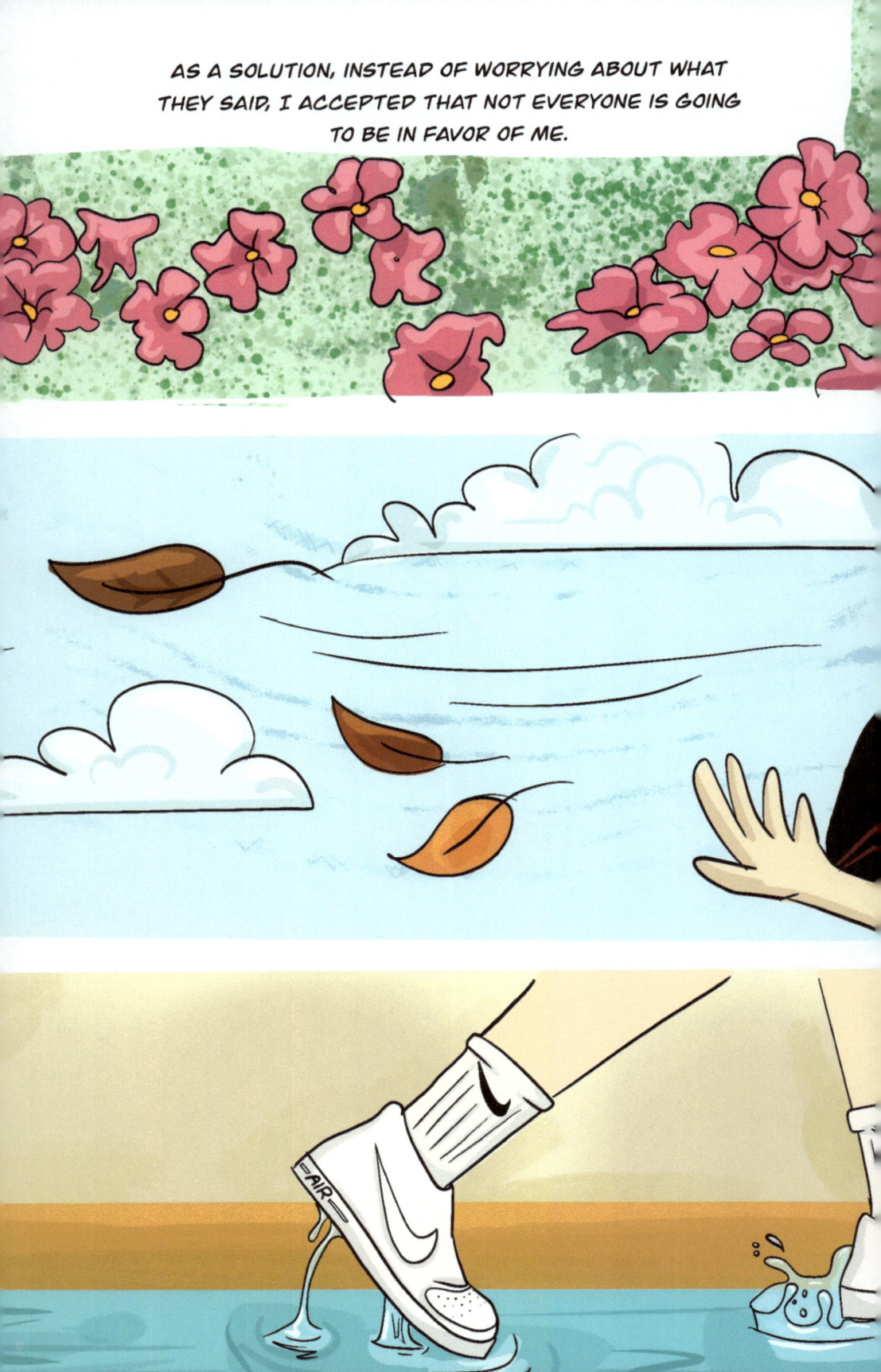

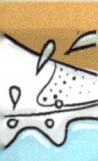

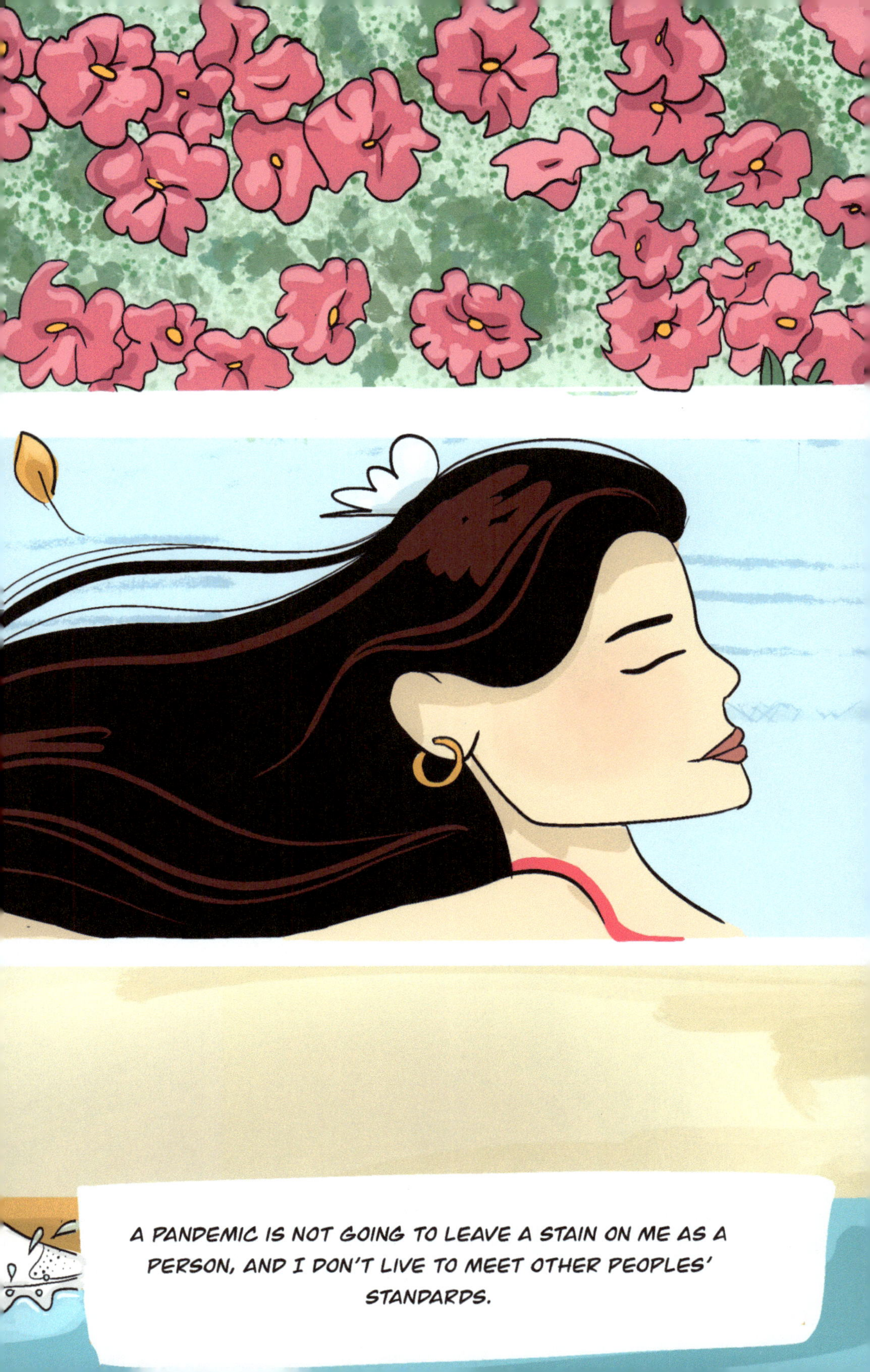

A PANDEMIC IS NOT GOING TO LEAVE A STAIN ON ME AS A PERSON, AND I DON'T LIVE TO MEET OTHER PEOPLES' STANDARDS.

NOT ASIAN ENOUGH

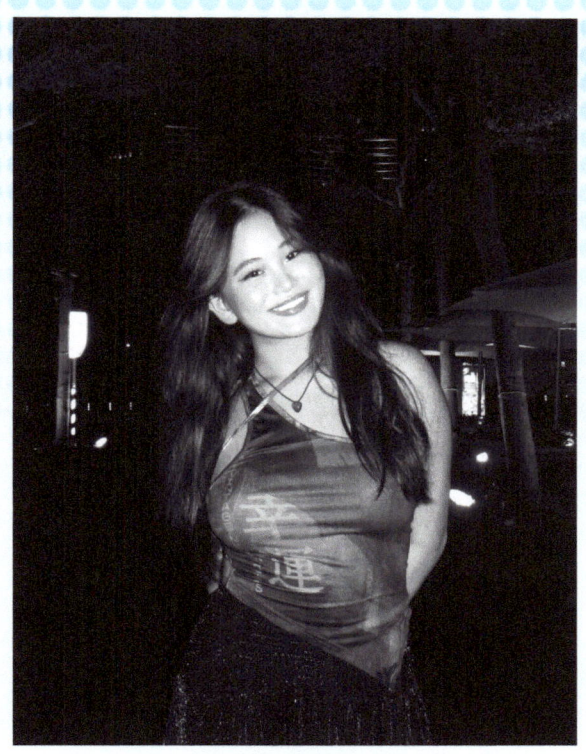

ALEXANDRA LAI

SHE STARTED OFF HER ARTISTIC CAREER WITH GOING
TO A NEARBY PARK AND DOODLING WHATEVER SHE
SAW. ALEXANDRA NEVER INTENDED TO WRITE AND
ILLUSTRATE A BOOK UNTIL SHE HAD TO DO SO FOR A
SECOND GRADER AS AN AP DRAWING PROJECT, BUT
SHE WANTED TO MAKE ONE ABOUT HER OWN JOURNEY
AND CHARACTER DEVELOPMENT

www.ingramcontent.com/pod-product-compliance
Lightning Source LLC
Chambersburg PA
CBHW040326010626
45792CB00024B/2171